CONTACT USA

A READING AND VOCABULARY TEXT

THIRD EDITION

PAUL ABRAHAM & DAPHNE MACKEY

Simmons College

University of Washington

Longman

Publisher: Mary Jane Peluso
Editor: Sheryl Olinsky
Development Editor: Margaret Grant
Production Editor: Noël Vreeland Carter
Interior Design: Noël Vreeland Carter,
    Wanda España, and Merle Krumper
Manufacturing Manager: Ray Keating
Art Director: Merle Krumper
Cover Design: Paul Polara
Art Production/Scanning: Marita Froimson
Charts: Warren Fischbach
Cover and Interior Art: Robert Kaufman

0-13-518754-0

CONTENTS

To the unsung professionals of ESL

CONTENTS

INTRODUCTION TO THE TEACHER

Contact U.S.A. is a reading and vocabulary text for high-beginning and low-intermediate ESL/EFL students. Although its structure and exercises are aimed primarily at developing academic reading skills and vocabulary, its content (a look at changes in values and lifestyles in the United States) is highly appropriate for all non-native English speakers, including immigrants, students in higher educational institutions, and students of English in foreign countries.

Changes in the new edition. This new edition includes individual work, pair work, and group work to expand the pre- and post-reading activities. Collaborative work expands the reading process by providing for new perspectives on the same text from other readers. Sharing ideas about the text that are related to reading adds a new dimension to the somewhat solitary process of reading. These activities also provide an opportunity to apply what is learned through reading to speaking and writing skills.

READING

Reading for high-beginning and low-intermediate students is sometimes a frustrating experience. Books that are appropriate in terms of the students' active English proficiency are often not challenging for adult readers, either in structure or content. Readings that match the student's intellectual or conceptual interest level usually have exercises requiring a more advanced active English proficiency. We have written this book on the premise that adult students at this level of English proficiency are able to read and understand more in English than they are able to produce actively. Therefore, although the readings may appear to be difficult for students at this level at first glance, the first analytical exercises are relatively simple, requiring less demanding reading and vocabulary skills. We feel that these types of reading and vocabulary skills are important for students to develop, particularly because the analysis of a reading beyond their proficiency level is a process that students confront in standardized tests in English. The reading exercises in this book progress from main idea to inference. The following is a general outline of each chapter.

CHAPTER OUTLINE

A FIRST LOOK

A. Background Building
B. Topic (skimming reading for topic of paragraphs)
C. Reading
D. Scanning/Vocabulary (similar–different analysis of vocabulary in the context of the reading)
E. Reading Comprehension (multiple choice)

LOOK AGAIN

A. Vocabulary (multiple choice)
B. Reading Comprehension (cloze summary or outline)
C. Think About It (active comprehension analysis of reading)
D. Reading (graphs or short readings related to the topic—can be used out of
        sequence in the chapter)

CONTACT A POINT OF VIEW

A. Background Building
B. Timed Reading (a personal observation followed by True, False, or Impossible
        to Know statements)
C. Vocabulary
D. React (semi-controlled discussion activities)
E. Word Analysis (Part 1: progressing through the book from recognition of
        function and form to production of appropriate forms;
        Part 2: stems and affixes)

LOOK BACK

A. Vocabulary (multiple choice)
B. Matching (synonyms)
C. Synthesis   (questions for discussion and suggestions for
        extension activities)
D. Vocabulary Preview

    The Instructor's Manual contains Vocabulary Review Tests and Answer Keys (both for chapter exercises and the review tests).

VOCABULARY

    This book was written with the firm belief that dictionaries are generally a reading inhibitor rather than a reading enhancer. With this in mind, the cardinal rule of the book is NO DICTIONARIES ALLOWED. The meaning of much of the vocabulary is implied within the reading passage, as the students discover when they complete the first vocabulary exercise, which requires them to analyze words within the context of the reading and compare them to other words that they already know. The vocabulary exercises and the inaccessibility of a dictionary force the students to look for meaning within the context, an essential reading skill. This book serves as a vocabulary builder because we reuse the vocabulary throughout the book so that students can recall vocabulary from previous chapters, where it is used in different context. This leads to actual acquisition of the words in the text.

CONTENT

From our experience as teachers, we feel that adult language learners need stimulating reading materials that (1) provide them with background information about American culture, (2) encourage their awareness of their environment, (3) prepare them to deal with the environment of the United States, and (4) let them draw their own conclusions about the United States. The presentation of information about the life and values in the United States is a very touchy subject; students are sensitive to "pro-America" rhetoric. In spite of this wariness, however, students want to understand some of the basic values and issues in the United States. We have chosen themes that have always generated a lot of discussion in class and about which students have strong opinions. The focus of these readings is primarily cross-cultural. The readings enable students and the teacher to examine American culture, to evaluate their feelings, and to redefine their positions in this culture and/or in their own cultures.

We have tried to present, as far as possible, an apolitical portrayal of the United States. The first reading in every chapter is general, giving the overall idea and the key vocabulary items connected to the subject. The timed reading is a personal point of view about some aspect of the subject. For example, the timed reading in the chapter on immigration is from the point of view of a native American. The chapter on race issues has a second reading about reverse discrimination. These points of view are closely tied in with the speaking activities in each chapter, encouraging students to express their ideas about the subject. Since these readings are our personal impressions, and are, as such, debatable, we encourage you to feel free to contribute your own personal points of view and to express your own cultural perspectives.

ACKNOWLEDGMENTS

Many people have given us feedback and suggestions on this and previous editions of Contact U.S.A. Several of the student surveys in the Background Building exercises were developed by Chérie Lenz-Hackett at the University of Washington.

Our thanks to Chérie and to the reviewers involved in this revision: Katsuko Asai, Regina Schlossberg, and Judy Jozaitis.

INTRODUCTION TO THE STUDENT

Contact U.S.A. has two purposes:

1. to improve your READING ability, and

2. to improve your VOCABULARY.

In this edition, you will have many opportunities to work with other students, in pairs and in small groups. Working with others and learning from each other is an important part of improving your reading skills and your general English language ability.

Each chapter in the book has the following sections.

A FIRST LOOK: exercises to determine general meaning of reading and vocabulary items

A. Background Building
B. Topic
C. Reading
D. Scanning/Vocabulary (similar/different)
E. Reading Comprehension

LOOK AGAIN: more detailed exercises in reading comprehension and vocabulary

A. Vocabulary
B. Reading Comprehension
C. Think about it
D. Reading

CONTACT A POINT OF VIEW: additional reading

A. Background Building
B. Timed Reading
C. Vocabulary
D. React
E. Word Analysis

LOOK BACK: review of the vocabulary from the chapter

A. Vocabulary
B. Matching
C. Synthesis
D. Vocabulary Preview

The first chapter, "Impressions of the United States," has special instructions for each exercise. These instructions will teach you how to use the book effectively.

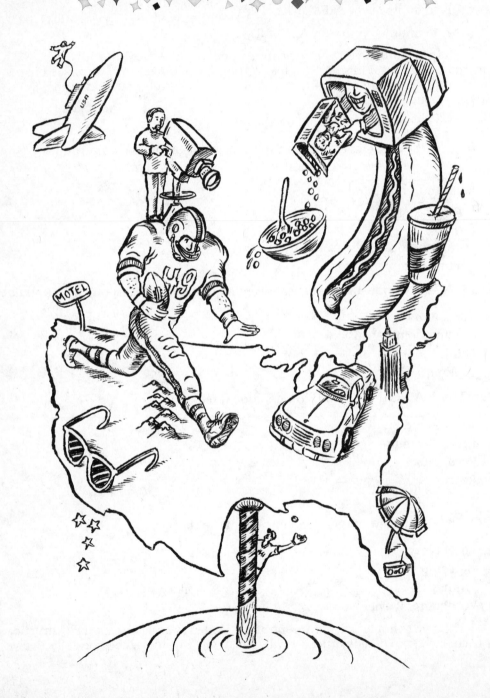

A FIRST LOOK

 BACKGROUND BUILDING

1. a. **Work on your own.** What are the first things you think of when you hear the words "United States?" What words come into your head? Write them here.

   Example: big, crowded streets

   b. **Work together.** Combine your list with a partner's list. Look at the combined list. Are the words *positive, negative,* or *neutral* (not positive or negative)? Write them again here.

Positive	Negative	Neutral
	crowded streets	big

   What were most of your words? Why?

2. a. **Work on your own.** What is in the illustration on page 2? Write the words here.

   b. **Work together.** Compare your list with a partner's. Why are these things in the picture? What other things do you think should be in the picture?

3. **Work on your own.** What would you like to learn about the United States?

B TOPIC

Before you begin to read, look at these topics. There is one topic for each paragraph. Look quickly at the reading to find these topics. Do not read every word at this point. Write the number of the paragraph next to the topic of that paragraph.

1. __2__ positive and negative ideas about the United States

2. _____ knowledge of a country

3. _____ this book about the United States

4. _____ first thoughts about the United States

5. __3__ how people form impressions

C READING

Now read, but try to think about groups of words, not individual words. Do not stop if you do not know the meaning of a word.

IMPRESSIONS OF THE UNITED STATES

1   The United States. What is your first thought when you hear these words?   1
Is it an image of something typically American?* Perhaps you think of   2
hamburgers and fast-food restaurants. Or perhaps you have an image of a   3
product, such as an American car or Coca-Cola.® Some people immediately   4
think of American universities. Others think of American companies. Many   5
Americans think of the red, white, and blue flag when they think of the United   6
States. There are many images associated with the name of a country.   7

2   There are also many ideas or concepts associated with the words *United*   8
States. Some people think of a positive concept, such as freedom, when they   9
think of the United States. Other people think of a negative concept, such as   10
American involvement in other countries. Many Americans have both positive   11
and negative ideas about their country. When they think of the lifestyle or the   12
scenery (landscapes such as mountains, or beaches at the ocean), they feel very   13
positive and proud of their country. But sometimes, when they think about the   14
government, they think about high taxes and international problems. Then they   15
have negative feelings about the country.   16

3   These images and ideas are all impressions of a country, the United States.   17
People form these impressions in many different ways They see American   18
products and advertisements. They read newspapers and hear people talk about   19
the United States. They probably see American movies and television shows.   20
These impressions are always changing. As people receive more information,   21
they adjust their images and concepts of a country.   22

4   Knowledge of a country includes many things. Typical products and actions   23
by governments are part of this knowledge. But the most important thing in   24
learning about a country is knowledge of the people of that country. What are   25
their customs and lifestyles? How do they raise their children? What are their   26
values and beliefs? How do they feel about work and entertainment, about time,   27
about friendships?   28

5   In this book you will read about many aspects of the United States. You   29
will read about lifestyles, institutions, values, and issues that are all part of   30
American life and culture. Before you begin each chapter, think of your own   31
impressions of the subject, such as American women, American cities, American   32
families. Use your own impressions to compare with and question the   33
impressions of the authors. Contact the U.S.A.   34

---

* Although technically more accurate, the term *North American* is not used by the
people in the United States to describe themselves. Therefore, the term *American* is
used throughout this book to describe things in the United States.

The following vocabulary exercise will help you to understand the meaning of new words in the reading without a dictionary.

 SCANNING/VOCABULARY

It is important to be able to find information quickly when you read. This is scanning. Scan the reading for these words. Write the number of the line where you find them.

Example: car ____4____   automobile __similar__

Now look at the word on the right. Is its meaning similar or different from the meaning of *car*? The meanings of *car* and *automobile* are similar, so you write **similar** on the line. Remember that the word similar does not mean exactly the same; it means that the two words are close in meaning.

Try another example:

first ____1____   last __different__

In this case, you find *first* in line 1 of the reading. The meanings are different, so you write **different** on the line. If you are not sure about the meaning of a word, read the sentence where you find it again. Try to understand its meaning from the other words in the sentence and the reading.

	LINE NUMBER		SIMILAR OR DIFFERENT?
1. thought	____	idea	____
2. image	____	picture	____
3. ideas	____	concepts	____
4. perhaps	____	maybe	____
5. positive	____	negative	____
6. scenery	____	landscapes	____
7. impressions	____	first ideas	____
8. form	____	make	____
9. includes	____	has inside	____
10. typical	____	common	____
11. products	____	customs	____
12. adjust	____	change a little	____
13. proud	____	ashamed	____
14. lifestyle	____	institutions	____
15. compare with	____	look at side by side	____

How much of the reading did you understand without using a dictionary? Do the next exercise to find out.

E ▸ READING COMPREHENSION

Circle the letter of the choice that best completes each sentence.

1. There are ___ examples given of images associated with the name United States.

   a. six   b. seven   c. eight

2. An example of a positive concept is ___.

   a. high taxes   b. freedom   c. advertisement

3. According to the reading, Americans are ___ about their lifestyle.

   a. scenery   b. negative   c. happy

4. According to the author, Americans ___ have negative thoughts about their country.

   a. always   b. never   c. sometimes

5. The author thinks that you, the reader, have ___ the United States already.

   a. no knowledge of   b. many   c. negative ideas about
                                impressions of

6. In paragraph 5, the author gives the idea that your ideas will ___.

   a. always be the   b. be wrong   c. sometimes be
      same as the author's   different from the
      ideas   author's ideas

7. The author thinks people probably have ___ impressions of American involvement in other countries.

   a. positive   b. negative   c. no

8. Foreign business people probably think of an American ___ when they hear the words United States.

   a. product   b. landscape   c. institution

9. The term *American* is used because ___.

   a. North American   b. people in the   c. the book is about
      is too long   United States   Canada
                                use it

10. People's impressions ___ when they learn more about a country.

    a. are negative   b. are never   c. change
                                different

LOOK AGAIN

Look at the correct answers for the vocabulary exercises (exercise D) in
"A First Look." Use the **similar** words to understand the meanings and to
answer this vocabulary exercise. If the words in the following exercise are
not in exercise D, look for them in the reading in order to understand their
meanings. Do not use a dictionary.

 A VOCABULARY

Circle the letter of the choice that best completes each sentence.

1. I want to know more about the ___ of the people: what they do every day
   and how they spend their free time.

   a. work   b. lifestyle   c. products

2. My mother and father work; ___ of my parents work.

   a. friendships   b. some   c. both

3. I am wearing a suit today because I want to make a good ___.

   a. involvement   b. custom   c. impression

4. Some people are happy about the changes, but ___ are unhappy.

   a. institutions b. personals   c. others

5. On the train I looked out the window at the ___.

   a. scenery   b. products   c. customs

6. There are many different ___ to the problem. It is not easy to
   understand.

   a. images   b. aspects   c. people

7. Schools and churches are ___.

   a. lifestyles   b. institutions   c. landscapes

8. My parents are very ___ of me when I make good grades at school.

   a. positive   b. concept   c. proud

B VOCABULARY/COMPREHENSION

Complete the reading by writing the correct choice on the line.

When people from other (1) _____ think about the United States,
  (a) institutions
  (b) lifestyles
  (c) countries

they probably have many different (2) _____. Some may have a(n)
  (a) impressions
  (b) aspects
  (c) products

(3) _____ of an American (4) _____ , such as a big car or
  (a) custom   (a) product
  (b) image   (b) aspect
  (c) landscape   (c) idea

a hamburger. Others may think of American (5) _____ , such as
  (a) impressions
  (b) institutions
  (c) lifestyles

universities.

People in the United States are proud of the beautiful (6) _____.
  (a) knowledge
  (b) scenery
  (c) impressions

They are also proud of the political (7) _____ they have in this
  (a) freedom
  (b) products
  (c) countries

country, but some are concerned about American involvement in other countries.

The authors think that the most important thing in learning about another

country is (8) _____ of the people in the country: their
  (a) country
  (b) knowledge
  (c) products

customs and (9) _____. They want the readers to think about
  (a) freedom
  (b) aspects
  (c) lifestyles

their own ideas and (10) _____ when they read the book.
  (a) aspects
  (b) scenery
  (c) impressions

 **THINK ABOUT IT**

Answer the following questions.

1. Ask several people from other countries this question: "What is your first thought when you hear the name of my country, _____?"

2. Do people ever have false impressions about your country or the people in your country? How are their ideas wrong?

3. What are some of the things you are proud of when you think of your country?

 READING

Do you ever wear blue jeans? When? Where were your blue jeans made? Read about blue jeans and answer the questions that follow.

Blue jeans are an example of an American product that is popular throughout the world. They were created by Levi Straus, a young German immigrant, in the 1850s in California. He made them for the gold miners there. The miners often ripped their pants at the knees and in the back because they had to kneel and bend looking for gold. Straus created a strong pair of overalls out of canvas, the material used for tents. He later used a cotton from France called *denim*. The denim was brought from France by ships with many Genoese sailors, from Genoa, Italy, in the crew. From this city's name came the name *jeans*.

Blue jeans were popular among cowboys in the Wild West and came to the East only after the 1930s. Later, in the 1950s, movie stars such as James Dean and Marlon Brando made jeans popular with American teenagers. In the 1970s, designers such as Calvin Klein and Gloria Vanderbilt made blue jeans popular with people of all ages.

Today people all over the world wear blue jeans, but the original idea came from the United States.

1. Who created the original blue jeans and why?

2. What were the first "jeans" made from?

3. Where does the name jeans come from?

4. Do people in your country know that jeans were first an American product? Do they wear American jeans or jeans made in your country or in other countries?

CONTACT A POINT OF VIEW

 BACKGROUND BUILDING

Complete these sentences.

1. When I first came to the United States, I was surprised because . . .

2. I was *not* surprised to see . . .

3. The thing which is most different for me in the U.S. is . . .

Reading quickly is a very important skill. Remember to read groups of words—do not stop on individual words. You must read *and* complete the first exercise in five minutes, so you need to read *very* quickly. The statements in the exercise contain information connected to the reading. This information is either *true* or *false*, or it is *impossible to know* (because the reading does not give the information).

B TIMED READING

Read the following point of view and answer the questions in five minutes.

I am from Thailand. I am a student in an American university. This is my third year in the United States. After three years, it is difficult to remember my first impressions of the United States. However, I noticed then and still notice now how much more informality there is in the United States than there is in Thailand.

Take, for example, clothes. I expected to see blue jeans because this is where they started, isn't it? But I didn't expect to see so many running shoes. People wear running shoes in classes, downtown, in expensive restaurants, and with business suits! I also couldn't believe the runners— *joggers* they call them—all over the place, but that gets into how Americans feel about health, which is another interesting topic.

If you think about the English language, you know that it is not a formal language. There is only one *you*—not a formal *you* for older people and an informal *you* for friends and children. I remember another thing that surprised me. My first English teacher in the United States was about fifty years old, but we called him *Al*, his first name. I wanted to call him *Mr. Al*, but he didn't like that. However, not all situations are informal like this; in business and in certain professions like medicine, things are more formal.

As a young person, I like the American idea of informality, but I think it will be better to be old in Thailand where people respect old people and have more formal relationships.

Read the following statements carefully to determine whether each is true (T), false (F), or impossible to know (ITK).

1. _____ The writer is a woman.

2. _____ The writer is a university student.

3. _____ Al was the teacher's last name.

4. _____ The writer is young.

5. _____ The writer is married.

6. _____ The writer never saw running shoes downtown.

7. _____ The writer lived in the city of San Francisco.

8. _____ Americans call doctors by their first name.

9. _____ The writer has more ideas about Americans and health.

10. _____ The writer thinks formality is better for old people.

C VOCABULARY

Circle the letter of the choice with the same meaning as the italicized word.

1. The way Americans feel about informality is an interesting *concept*.

   a. information   b. idea   c. aspect

2. I *noticed* a person sitting alone in the restaurant.

   a. saw   b. talked to   c. called

3. I know a lot of *runners*.

   a. bicycles   b. office people   c. joggers

4. They had a very old *friendship*.

   a. kind of relationship   b. understanding   c. belief

5. I have a good *impression* of her.

   a. general idea   b. custom   c. friendship

6. I never *start* my homework until 10:00 P.M.

   a. end   b. begin   c. try

7. Please give me *more* information.

   a. additional   b. good   c. better

8. I never *question* my father's ideas.

   a. answer   b. understand   c. ask about with doubt

9. This is an interesting *thought*.

   a. issue   b. quick idea   c. feeling

10. When my mother telephoned, I *immediately* told her the news.

    a. at the first moment   b. generally   c. slowly

D REACT

Answer these questions. Discuss them with a classmate.

1. What are some examples of informality?

2. Is your country formal or informal?

3. Do you think formality or informality is better? Why? In what situations?

E WORD ANALYSIS

PART 1

What shorter words can you see in these words?

Example: runner ___run___

1. lifestyle _____ _____

2. informality _____

3. homemaker _____ _____

4. landscape _____

5. newspaper _____ _____

6. comparison _____

7. freedom _____

8. production _____

9. friendship _____

10. knowledge _____

11. action _____

12. advertisement _____

PART 2

Read the following information about nouns and adjectives, and then complete the exercise. Decide whether the italicized words are nouns or adjectives.

A **noun** is a word used to name something. For example, *girl, box, idea,* and *restaurant* are all nouns.

An **adjective** gives some information about a noun. For example, *good, interesting,* and *green* are all adjectives when they describe a noun.

	NOUN	ADJECTIVE
1. I live in a *small* apartment.	____	√
2. *English* is difficult.	____	____
3. I am studying *English* history.	____	____
4. That is a *great* idea!	____	____
5. Many good things in life are *free.*	____	____
6. I have a *negative* feeling about politics.	____	____
7. *Good* friends are life's greatest pleasure.	____	____
8. I never read the *newspaper* here.	____	____
9. Is that a typical *product* of your country?	____	____
10. My aunt is one of the *friendliest* people I know.	____	____

LOOK BACK

 A VOCABULARY

Circle the letter of the choice that best completes each sentence.

1. I think that business is the best __ to get into.
   a. lifestyle   b. profession   c. thought

2. My friend teaches in elementary school because she enjoys __ with children.
   a. involvement   b. production   c. impressions

3. I am interested in this car because I saw the __.
   a. impressions   b. advertisement   c. flags

4. It is difficult to talk about __ in English.
   a. actions   b. concepts   c. institutions

5. I like the __ in the mountains better than at the ocean.
   a. scenery   b. comparison   c. positive

6. What do you do for __? Do you go to movies or stay at home?
   a. work   b. entertainment   c. association

7. I study at an English language __.
   a. situation   b. institute   c. profession

8. When you travel long distances, it is difficult to __ the time differences.
   a. notice   b. adjust to   c. involve

9. I don't have any __ about the trip to New York.
   a. information   b. aspects   c. images

10. He did some very strange things. His __ frightened me.
    a. aspects   b. thoughts   c. actions

B MATCHING

Find the word or phrase in column B that has a similar meaning to a word in column A. Write the letter of that word or phrase next to the word in column A.

	A		B
1. _d_	immediately		a. something made
2. _g_	thought		b. good
3. ___	product		c. participation or association with
4. ___	adjust		d. right away
5. ___	jogger		e. scenery
6. ___	lifestyle		f. change
7. ___	positive		g. idea
8. ___	landscape		h. way of life
9. ___	perhaps		i. maybe
10. ___	involvement		j. runner

C SYNTHESIS

Work together. *Read the following three tasks and choose the one that interests you most. Join group 1, 2, or 3 to work on the task.*

1. **Careful Observation.** Decide as a group where to observe Americans—perhaps at a bank, at a supermarket, or in your dormitory. Go to that place to observe how people dress, how they interact, and how they get around.

2. **Questions about the United States.** Decide as a group on three specific questions about the United States that you would like to ask Americans. Each group member should interview at least two Americans.

3. **Survey.** Ask Americans about their impressions about other countries. For example, ask, "What is the first thing you think of when you hear the names of these countries/cities: Thailand, Rio de Janeiro, etc. . . .?"

Report your findings to the whole class.

D VOCABULARY PREVIEW

What shorter words can you see in these words from Chapter 2?

1. mixture   _mix_
2. background   _____ _____
3. downfall   _____ _____
4. cowboys   _____ _____
5. unwilling   _____
6. western   _____
7. neighborhood   _____
8. ownership   _____
9. reservation   _____
10. racial   _____

2 A COUNTRY OF IMMIGRANTS

A FIRST LOOK

 BACKGROUND BUILDING

1. Ask your classmates questions about the illustration on page 20.

2. The title of this chapter is "A Country of Immigrants." What kinds of people come to the U. S.? Where are they from? When did they come to this country? Why did they come? Complete this chart. Compare your information with a classmate's information.

NAME OF PEOPLE	NAME OF COUNTRY	WHY THEY CAME
_____	_____	_____
_____	_____	_____
_____	_____	_____

B TOPIC

Before you begin to read, look at these topics. There is one topic for each paragraph. Look quickly at the reading to find these topics. Do not read every word at this point. Write the number of the paragraph next to the topic of that paragraph.

1. _____ examples of different types of neighborhoods

2. _____ the different faces of immigrants in the United States

3. _____ diversity in American society

4. _____ history of immigration in the United States

Now read.

A COUNTRY OF IMMIGRANTS

1   As you walk along the street in any American city, you see many different   1
faces. You see faces from Central and South America, from Asia, from Africa,   2
and from Europe. These are the faces of the United States, a country of   3
immigrants from all over the world. Immigrants are people who leave one   4
country to live permanently in another country.   5

2   Northern Europeans from countries such as England and Holland first   6
came to North America in the 1600s. These people generally had light skin and   7
light hair. They came to live in North America because they wanted religious   8
freedom. In the 1700s and early 1800s, immigrants continued to move from   9
Europe to the United States. At this time, there was one group of unwilling   10
immigrants, Africans. These people were tricked or forced to come to the   11
United States, where they worked on large farms in the South. The blacks had   12
no freedom; they were slaves. In the 1800s, many German, Scandinavian,   13
Chinese, and Irish immigrants came to the United States. They came because of   14
economic or political problems in their countries. The most recent immigrants   15
to the United States, people from Asia, the Caribbean, Latin America, and   16
Eastern Europe, also came because of economic or political problems in their   17
own countries. Most of these immigrants thought of the United States as a land   18
of opportunity, as a chance for freedom and new lives.   19

3   In the United States, these immigrants looked for assistance from other   20
immigrants who shared the same background, language, and religion. Therefore,   21
there are neighborhoods in each U.S. city with almost all one homogeneous   21
ethnic group. There are mostly Italian, Puerto Rican, or Irish neighborhoods in   23
many East Coast cities and mostly Mexican neighborhoods in the Southwest. In   24
Dearborn, Michigan, there is a large group of Lebanese. There are racial   25
neighborhoods, such as Chinatown in San Francisco and Harlem, an African   26
American neighborhood, in New York. There are also neighborhoods with a   27
strong religious feeling such as a Jewish part of Brooklyn in New York. And, of   28
course, there are economic neighborhood divisions; in American cities very   29
often poor people do not live in the same neighborhoods as rich people.   30

4   This diversity of neighborhoods in the cities is a reflection of the different   31
groups in American society. American society is a mixture of racial, language,   32
cultural, religious, and economic groups. So much diversity is sometimes difficult,   33
but many people enjoy it. They think diversity enriches their lives.   34

REACT

Is there some information in the reading that you want to know more about? Underline the sentence(s) where you find this information. Talk to your classmates and teacher about it.

 ## D SCANNING/VOCABULARY

*Scan the reading for these words. Write the number of the line where you find each word. Then compare its meaning in the sentence to the meaning of the word(s) on the right. Are the words similar or different? Write **similar** or **different** on the line.*

	LINE NUMBER		SIMILAR OR DIFFERENT?
1. world	4	globe	similar
2. immigrants		tourists	
3. such as		for example	
4. generally		usually	
5. unwilling		willing	
6. slaves		free people	
7. recent		close to now	
8. economic		financial	
9. opportunity		chance	
10. assistance		help	
11. shared		had together	
12. mostly		completely	
13. homogeneous		all the same	
14. poor		rich	
15. diversity		variety	
16. enriches		makes poor	
17. difficult		easy	

READING COMPREHENSION

Circle the letter of the choice that best completes each sentence.

1. Two people of the same race share the same __.
   a. language   b. religion   c. color

2. The first immigrants in the United States were __.
   a. black   b. religious people   c. Indochinese

3. The first Africans in North America were __ immigrants.
   a. happy   b. unwilling   c. recent

4. Harlem is an example of a __ neighborhood.
   a. religious   b. language   c. racial

5. Immigrants moved __ other immigrants from their countries.
   a. close to   b. far away from   c. without

6. The most recent immigrants came because of __ problems.
   a. racial   b. religious   c. political

7. There __ rich and poor people in the same neighborhoods in the United States.
   a. are often   b. are not usually   c. are never

8. The topic of the third paragraph is __.
   a. immigration   b. American society   c. neighborhoods in American cities

9. There were more __ immigrants in the East than in the West.
   a. Irish   b. Chinese   c. Mexican

10. American society is __.
    a. not diverse   b. diverse   c. homogeneous

LOOK AGAIN

A VOCABULARY

Circle the letter of the choice that best completes each sentence.

1. Assistance is __.
   a. religion   b. work   c. help

2. The East Coast and the Southwest are __ of(in) the country.
   a. groups of people   b. parts   c. cities

3. An example of religion is __.
   a. Jewish   b. black   c. Italian

4. A neighborhood is __.
   a. an apartment   b. a house   c. a city division
      building

5. A society is __.
   a. a group of people   b. immigrants   c. all American

6. An example of race is __.
   a. Roman Catholic   b. white   c. Irish

7. A government problem is a __ problem.
   a. political   b. street   c. forced

8. English is a __.
   a. language   b. religion   c. literature

9. A minute is a __ of an hour.
   a. mixture   b. group   c. division

10. A person with a lot of money is __.
    a. economic   b. rich   c. poor

B READING COMPREHENSION

Complete this outline of the reading.

1. Introduction

   You see many different (1) _____ on the streets in the United

   States because it is a country of (2) _____.

2. Immigrants

   The first immigrants: from (3) _____.

   A group of unwilling immigrants: (4) _____.

   In the 1800s, (5) _____ came because of

   (6) _____ problems. The most recent immigrants,

   (7) _____ , came because of

   (8) _____ problems.

3. Neighborhoods

   On the East Coast, there are neighborhoods of mostly (9) _____.

   In the Southwest, there are mostly (10) _____ neighborhoods. In

   San Francisco and New York, (11) _____ and

   (12) _____ are examples of neighborhoods made up of almost

   all one race. An example of a religious neighborhood is in

   (13) _____ , where most of the people are (14) _____.

4. Conclusion: Circle your choice.

   The writer thinks that the diversity in American society is sometimes

   (15) *easy/difficult*, but many people think that it is interesting.

THINK ABOUT IT

Answer the following questions.

1. Think about immigrants or refugees in your area. Where do you they live? Do they live near other people with the same background? The same language? The same religion?

2. Think of a neighborhood in a city in your country or in the United States and answer these questions.

   Name or location of the neighborhood: _____

   _____

   Is this neighborhood mixed or homogeneous? _____

   _____

   Type of people who live there: _____

   _____

3. What is the neighborhood like where you live?

Look at Figures 1 and 2, and answer the questions.

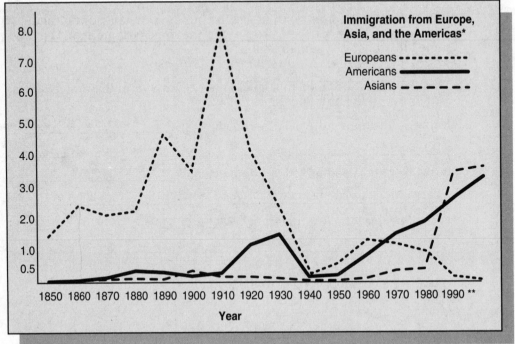

Source: U.S. Statistical Abstracts
*numbers in millions
**estimated
Americans = people from North America, Central America, and South America

FIGURE 1

1. What information does Figure 1 show?

2. Which group has had the most immigrants to the U.S.—people from Europe, Asia, or the Americas?

3. Between 1850 and 1860, about how many Europeans immigrated to the United States?

4. During what period was there the greatest amount of immigration?

5. During which period was European immigration lower than immigration
   (a) from the Americas?   (b) from Asia?

6. According to Figure 1, which group has the most immigrants now?

COUNTRY OF ORIGIN OF THE LARGEST NUMBER OF IMMIGRANTS IN 1992			
1. Mexico	213,800	6. China (PRC)	38,900
2. Vietnam	77,700	7. India	36,600
3. Philippines	61,000	8. El Salvador	26,200
4. Former Soviet Union	43,600	9. Poland	25,200
5. Dominican Republic	42,000	10. United Kingdom	20,000

Statistical Abstracts of the United States, 1994.

FIGURE 2

1. Where did the most immigrants come from in 1992—Europe, Asia, or the Americas?
2. What surprises you about this list?

CONTACT A POINT OF VIEW

 BACKGROUND BUILDING

1. What does the illustration above show?

2. What do you know about the history of native Americans in the United States?

B TIMED READING

Read the following point of view and answer the questions in five minutes.

My name is Haske Noswood. I am a native American, a Navajo. You probably know native Americans as "Indians" and associate us with cowboys and western movies.

Most people forget that we were the first Americans, that we were here before any white men. Once, the Navajo and other native American groups lived well. Some of us hunted; some of us farmed. Most of us moved from place to place according to the season. We did not believe in land ownership. We believed that land belonged to all people.

The white people thought differently. They came to our lands and divided it up among themselves. They took our land. We did not understand until it was too late. They tricked us and forced us all onto these reservations. They "gave" us this reservation land.

There is reservation land all over the country. There is the Hopi reservation in Arizona and the Cherokee reservation in Tennessee. But this reservation land is almost always the worst land. They often put us on land that no one else wanted. A lot of people have left the reservation to get good jobs or an education, but I am staying on the reservation because my people have many problems and I want to help them.

Read the following statements carefully to determine whether each is true (T), false (F), or impossible to know (ITK).

1. _____ A reservation is a city.

2. _____ The Navajo reservation is in New Mexico.

3. _____ The Cherokee reservation is in Arizona.

4. _____ High taxes are one of the problems on the reservation.

5. _____ There are few opportunities for work on the reservation.

6. _____ Haske Noswood lives in New Mexico.

7. _____ All native Americans live in one area of the country.

8. _____ The reservation land is often bad land.

9. _____ Each native American owned a piece of land.

10. _____ Haske is a hunter.

C VOCABULARY

Circle the letter of the word(s) with the same meaning as the italicized word.

1. What is the *real* problem?
   a. true   b. bad   c. difficult

2. I was *once* a farmer.
   a. never   b. always   c. at one time

3. This is *the worst* weather! It is really cold.
   a. very bad   b. very difficult c. amazing

4. Spending money was my *downfall*.
   a. happiness   b. opportunity   c. biggest problem

5. He did *poorly* on his test.
   a. badly   b. well   c. hard

6. We will *divide* the house into apartments.
   a. sell   b. cut up   c. live

7. The farming *season* in the north is very short.
   a. place   b. time of year   c. area

8. I will *call* the baby John.
   a. number   b. tell   c. name

9. I *force* myself to study.
   a. push   b. continue   c. walk

10. I live *well* but I have little money.
    a. in a good way b. poorly   c. hard

D REACT

Share your ideas with a classmate or with the class. Answer the following questions.

1. Who were the first people in your country?

2. How many different groups of people are there in your country now?

3. What is(are) the language(s) in your country?

4. What is(are) the race(s) in your country?

5. What is(are) the religion(s) in your country?

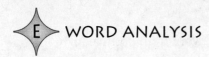

PART 1

Are the italicized words used as nouns or as adjectives?

	NOUN	ADJECTIVE
1. Salt is an *ingredient* used in cooking.	____	____
2. That is quite a *wealthy* neighborhood.	____	____
3. What is your *problem*?	____	____
4. He is a *native* of the United States.	____	____
5. My *native* language is English.	____	____
6. There is a large *group* of people outside.	____	____
7. What's the *difference*?	____	____
8. This is *your* book, isn't it?	____	____
9. What *color* is your hair?	____	____
10. My eyes are *brown*.	____	____

PART 2

1. a. These prefixes change the meaning of a word from positive to negative.

   Can you think of another example?

un-	willing	**un**willing	_____
in-	formal	**in**formal	_____
im-	possible	**im**possible	_____
dis-	agree	**dis**agree	_____

1. b. Study the meanings of these prefixes.

   | hetero- | different | **hetero**geneous | _____ |
   | homo- | same | **homo**geneous | _____ |

   The population in the United States is **heterogeneous**. In Japan, the population is more **homogeneous**.

2. Complete the sentences with one of the words from 1a or 1b.

   a. Our class is a(n) _____ group. We have students from many different countries.

   b. Slaves were _____ immigrants to the United States.

   c. Our ideas are completely different. I _____ with you.

   d. I can't do that. I'm sorry, but it's _____.

   e. I have a(n) _____ lifestyle, so I don't have very many dressy clothes. I usually wear pants and a sweater.

   f. In that new neighborhood, the people are all similar—they all have about the same income and are about the same age. They even drive the same kinds of cars. It's too _____ for me!

LOOK BACK

 A **VOCABULARY**

Circle the letter of the choice that best completes each sentence.

1. I don't want to say anything. I am __ to speak.
   a. strong   b. permanent   c. unwilling

2. A group of people with many different religions, languages, and races is a __ group.
   a. racial   b. cultural   c. mixed

3. He is a complete stranger to me. I don't know anything about his __.
   a. concept   b. background   c. assistance

4. Good friends __ a person's life.
   a. enjoy   b. force   c. enrich

5. A class is a __ of students.
   a. group   b. neighborhood   c. reflection

6. I want to buy the apartment building. Then I will be the __.
   a. neighbor   b. assistant   c. owner

7. I came to this __ because I wanted to live in a different area.
   a. place   b. mixture   c. division

8. He __ lives here. He moved out of town last month.
   a. no longer   b. supposedly   c. permanently

9. She is a very __ person. She goes to church twice a week.
   a. unwilling   b. political   c. religious

10. I like everything about my apartment __ the cost. It is too expensive.
    a. with   b. except for   c. entirely

B MATCHING

Find the word or phrase in column B that has a similar meaning to a word or phrase in column A. Write the letter of that word or phrase next to the word in column A.

	A		B
1. _____	opportunity		a. an area of a town or city
2. _____	varied		b. have together
3. _____	except for		c. chance
4. _____	entirely		d. try to find
5. _____	such as		e. name
6. _____	look for		f. all
7. _____	neighborhood		g. but
8. _____	recent		h. for example
9. _____	call		i. close to the present
10. _____	share		j. diverse

 C SYNTHESIS

Work together.

1. Interview other people (a classmate, your teacher, a neighbor). Ask them about their background: where they were born; where their families were from; etc. . . . Work with your classmates to write interview questions.

2. Diversity is common in many countries in the world. What are some positive aspects to diversity? What are some negative aspects?

3. Find out more about native Americans. Go to the library or a museum. Find out the name of a native American group. What language(s) do they speak? What are their beliefs? How do they live today?

D VOCABULARY PREVIEW

What shorter words can you see in these words from Chapter 3?

1. employment   _employ_
2. movement   _____
3. countless   _____ _____
4. improvement   _____
5. entertainment   _____
6. apartment   _____
7. unlike   _____
8. revitalize   _____
9. reconstruction   _____
10. rebuild   _____
11. government   _____
12. alive   _____

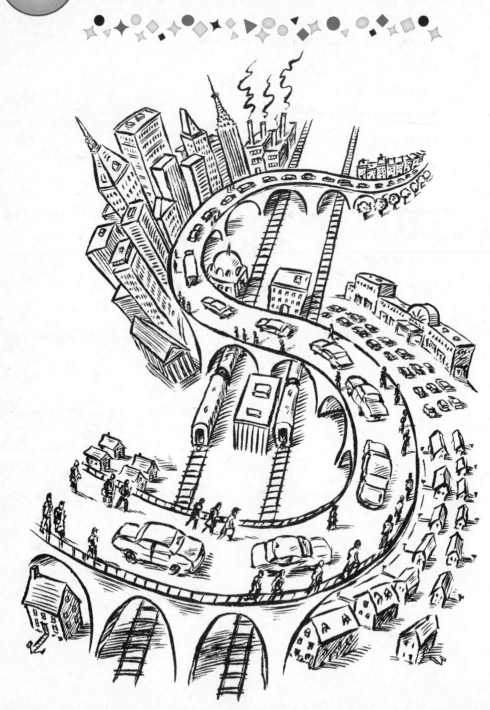

A FIRST LOOK

 BACKGROUND BUILDING

1. **Work on your own.** Where do you come from? From a city? From the suburbs (just outside the city) or from the country (far from a city)?

2. **Work together.** This chapter is about cities in America, but cities everywhere are similar. Write some impressions you have when you think about cities.

3. Which of your impressions are positive? Which are negative? Neutral?

B TOPIC

Before you begin to read, look at these topics. There is one topic for each paragraph. Look quickly at the reading to find these topics. Do not read every word at this point. Write the number of the paragraph next to the topic of that paragraph.

1. _____ population information

2. _____ cities are living again

3. _____ where people are moving now

4. _____ a description of cities

5. _____ a house in the suburbs

6. _____ a new type of city resident

7. _____ results of the move back to the cities

Now read.

CITIES IN AMERICA

1   American cities are similar to other cities around the world: In every   1
country, cities reflect the values of the culture. Cities contain the very best   2
aspects of a society: opportunities for education, employment, and entertainment. 3
They also contain the very worst parts of a society: violent crime, racial conflict, 4
and poverty. American cities are changing, just as American society is changing. 5

2   After World War II, the population of most large American cities decreased;   6
however, the population in many Sun Belt cities (those of the South and West)   7
increased. Los Angeles and Houston are cities where population increased. These   8
population shifts (the movement of people) to and from the city reflect the   9
changing values of American society.   10

3   During this time, in the late 1940s and early 1950s, city residents became   11
wealthier, more prosperous. They had more children so they needed more space.   12
They moved out of their apartments in the city to buy their own homes. They   13
bought houses in the suburbs (areas without many offices or factories near cities). 14
During the 1950s, the American "dream" was to have a house in the suburbs.   15

4   Now things are changing. The children of the people who left the cities in   16
the 1950s are now adults. Many, unlike their parents, want to live in the cities. 17
Some continue to move to cities in the Sun Belt. Cities are expanding, and the   18
population is increasing in such states as Texas, Florida, and California. Others are 19
moving to older, more established cities of the Northeast and Midwest, such as   20
Boston, Baltimore, and Chicago. The government, industry, and individuals are   21
restoring old buildings, revitalizing poor neighborhoods, and rebuilding forgotten 22
areas of these cities.   23

5   Many young professionals, doctors, lawyers, and executives, are moving back 24
into the city. Many are single; others are married, but often without children. They 25
prefer the city to the suburbs because their jobs are there; or they just enjoy the 26
excitement and opportunities that the city offers. A new class is moving into the 27
cities—a wealthier, more mobile class.   28

6   This population shift is bringing problems as well as benefits. Countless poor 29
people must leave their apartments in the city because the owners want to sell   30
the buildings or make condominiums, apartments that people buy instead of rent.   31
In the 1950s, many poor people did not have enough money to move to the   32
suburbs; now many of these same people do not have enough money to stay in   33
the cities.   34

7   Only a few years ago, people thought that the older American cities were   35
dying. Some city residents now see a bright, new future. Others see only   37
problems and conflicts. One thing is sure: many dying cities are alive again.   38

REACT

In the reading, choose one sentence that you find interesting and write it here. Talk about its meaning with a partner.

 D SCANNING/VOCABULARY

PART 1

Write the line number where you find the word. Then circle the letter of the choice with the best meaning for the word as it is used in that sentence.

1. reflect   line number __
   a. consider   b. shine   c. mirror

2. aspects   line number __
   a. benefits   b. sides   c. concepts

3. opportunities   line number __
   a. places   b. chances   c. needs

4. conflict   line number __
   a. opposition   b. peace   c. issue

5. violent   line number __
   a. using force   b. peaceful   c. difficult

6. space   line number __
   a. yards   b. land   c. room

7. restoring   line number __
   a. rebuilding   b. destroying   c. building stores in

8. countless   line number __
   a. a few   b. many   c. homeless

9. shift   line number __
   a. drive   b. change   c. action

10. alive   line number __
    a. interesting   b. revitalized   c. dying

PART 2

Find a word that is the opposite of the one given. The line where you will find the word is given.

1. line 4   best   _____
2. line 5   wealth   _____
3. line 6   increased   _____
4. line 12   poorer   _____
5. line 14   city   _____
6. line 17   similar to   _____
7. line 18   growing smaller   _____
8. line 22   destroying   _____
9. line 27   boredom   _____
10. line 38 alive   _____

E   READING COMPREHENSION

Circle the letter of the choice that best completes each sentence.

1. The author thinks that cities all over the world are __.
   a. the same   b. similar   c. different

2. In paragraph 1, the author says that some good aspects of cities are schools, __, and things to do.
   a. values   b. jobs   c. changes

3. The author gives __ examples of the worst parts of a culture.
   a. two   b. three   c. four

4. The population of most large American cities __ after World War II.
   a. decreased   b. increased   c. remained the same

5. The population in Houston and Los Angeles, __ the population in most other cities, increased after the war.
   a. similar to   b. unlike   c. as well as

6. City residents became wealthier and more prosperous __ World War II.
   a. during   b. after   c. before

7. In the 1950s, many city residents wanted to __.
   a. live in the suburbs   b. revitalize the city   c. live in apartments

8. Many people are now __ the cities.
   a. moving from   b. leaving   c. returning to

9. A few years ago, the cities were __.
   a. alive   b. dying   c. entertaining

10. In paragraph 7, the author talks about the __ of cities.
    a. bright future   b. benefits   c. opportunities

LOOK AGAIN

A VOCABULARY

Circle the letter of the choice that best completes each sentence.

1. The problem of divorce has many different __.
   a. opportunities   b. benefits   c. aspects

2. The United States is a wealthy nation, but there is still __ here.
   a. space   b. opportunity   c. poverty

3. I don't like living with a roommate. I'm moving __ my family's house.
   a. back to   b. from   c. out of

4. She is __ her sister; she is very tall and her sister is very short.
   a. similar to   b. unlike   c. like

5. One benefit of living in this apartment is that it has more __.
   a. aspects   b. space   c. shifts

6. This box __ many old books and souvenirs.
   a. reflects   b. explains   c. contains

7. The population of the world __ daily.
   a. increases   b. inflates   c. decreases

8. Please don't __ yet. It's still early.
   a. stay   b. leave   c. shift

9. Do you __ your apartment, or is it a condominium?
   a. shift   b. rent   c. buy

10. He has no job; he is looking for __.
    a. excitement   b. employment   c. entertainment

B READING COMPREHENSION

Mark these events in the order that they happened. Number 1 happened first, number 2 happened second, and so on through number 10.

a. _____ They had large families.

b. _____ They moved to the suburbs.

c. _____ World War II ended.

d. _____ They wanted houses of their own.

e. _____ City residents became wealthier.

f. _____ Their children grew up.

g. _____ They wanted to live in the cities.

h. _____ They are rebuilding many cities.

i. _____ They are returning to the cities.

j. _____ They needed more space.

C THINK ABOUT IT

Work on your own. *Answer the following questions.*

1. Where do you find the following? In a city? The suburbs? The country? In all three?

   a. opportunities for good education   _____

   b. condominiums   _____

   c. quiet, open space   _____

   d. factories   _____

   e. a lot of crime   _____

   f. racial conflict   _____

   g. high cost of living   _____

   h. opportunities for employment   _____

   i. entertainment   _____

   j. big houses   _____

2. Where do you want to live in the future? In the city? In the suburbs? Or in the country?

3. What is important for you in this decision? Put number 1 next to the most important item, number 2 next to the second most important, and so forth.

_____ a lot of space   _____ convenience

_____ educational opportunities   _____ good apartments or houses

_____ entertainment and action   _____ beautiful scenery

_____ cost of living   ___2___ interesting people

_____ friendly neighbors   _____ (other) _____

_____ very little crime   _____

Work together. *Compare your answers to those of others in a small group of three or four. Report to the class.*

D CHART READING

Look carefully at the chart of the population of eight cities in the United States (Figure 3). Answer the questions below.

1. Which of these cities had the largest population in 1970?

_____

2. Which of these cities had the smallest population in 1970?

_____

3. In which cities did the population increase in both 1980 and 1990?

_____

4. In which cities did the population decrease in both 1980 and 1990?

_____

5. In which cities did the population decrease in 1980 and increase in 1990?

_____

City Population Chart: Eight U.S. Cities			
	1970	1980	1990	Percent (%) change 1980-1990
Baltimore	905,000	787,000	736,000	-6.4
Boston	641,000	563,000	574,000	2.0
Chicago	3,369,000	3,005,000	2,784,000	-7.4
Detroit	1,514,000	1,203,000	1,028,000	-14.6
Houston	1,234,000	1,595,000	1,631,000	2.2
Los Angeles	2,812,000	2,967,000	3,485,000	17.4
Miami	335,000	347,000	359,000	3.5
Seattle	531,000	494,000	516,000	4.5

FIGURE 3

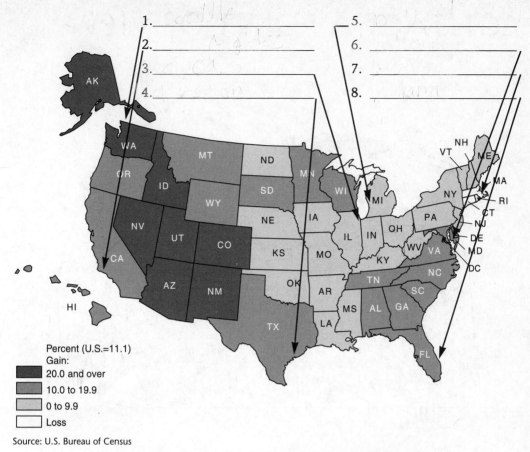

1._____
2._____
3._____
4._____

5._____
6._____
7._____
8._____

Percent (U.S.=11.1)
Gain:
- ■ 20.0 and over
- ■ 10.0 to 19.9
- □ 0 to 9.9
- □ Loss

Source: U.S. Bureau of Census

Projected Percent Change in State Population: 1990 to 2000

FIGURE 4

On the map of the United States above, locate each of the eight cities in the chart on the previous page, and write its name on the line. The map shows projected population change from 1990 to 2000 in the states where these cities are located. Write two facts that this map tells you.

1._____

2._____

How many of the states can you name where the population has increased more than 20 percent? Write them below.

_____   _____

_____   _____

_____   _____

_____   _____

CONTACT A POINT OF VIEW

 BACKGROUND BUILDING

Work together. *Look at the two buildings in the picture. Write as many words as you can to describe the two buildings.*

CONDOMINIUMS FOR SALE   APARTMENTS FOR RENT

1. _____   1. _____

2. _____   2. _____

3. _____   3. _____

4. _____   4. _____

Where do most people live in major cities in your country? In houses? In apartments? Can you buy apartments? Apartments that you buy are called *condominiums* in the United States, and they have become very popular recently.

TIMED READING

Read the following point of view, and answer the questions in four minutes.

Charlotte and Harry Johnson grew up in the city. They were neighbors as children, fell in love, and got married. They live in an apartment in their old neighborhood on the south side of town. They have two children, both boys. Harry is a bus driver, and Charlotte is a waitress at a neighborhood restaurant.

Mr. Harley, their landlord, bought the apartment building back in the 1920s. The building is getting old now, and Mr. Harley wants to sell it and retire. A Mr. Chin wants to buy the building and make condominiums. He offered Mr. Harley $950,000 for the building. Mr. Harley wants to sell, but he's worried about the Johnsons. They're like family. He even knew their families before Harry and Charlotte were born. He knows they don't have the money to buy a condominium. He says, "The boys are like my own grandchildren. What can I do?"

Mr. Chin, of Chin Development Corporation, is a very important force in the revitalization of the south side of town. His company rebuilt the old factory area—a forgotten section of town. His work is bringing new residents and business to the south side. The Chin Development Corporation wants to buy the old apartment building from Mr. Harley. Mr. Chin is offering him a good price for the building. Of course, after reconstruction, the value of the building will increase greatly. "These people don't seem to want progress or improvements. We have to bring new, wealthier residents to the city to keep it alive."

Read the following statements carefully to determine whether each is true (T), false (F), or impossible to know (ITK).

1. _____ Charlotte and Harry lived in this neighborhood when they were children.

2. _____ They have two sons.

3. _____ Charlotte works in the neighborhood.

4. _____ Mr. Chin is offering nine hundred and fifteen thousand dollars for the building.

5. _____ The Johnsons like Mr. Harley's family.

6. _____ Mr. Harley has no children.

7. _____ Mr. Chin wants to rent the apartments.

8. _____ He revitalized only the north side of the city.

9. _____ Mr. Harley bought the building in 1925.

10. _____ After reconstruction, the value of the building will decrease.

C VOCABULARY

Circle the letter of the choice with the same meaning as the italicized word(s).

1. Mr. Harley is the *landlord.*
   a. renter   b. owner   c. custodian
2. The building is *getting* old.
   a. taking   b. shifting   c. becoming
3. He *is worried* about the Johnsons.
   a. doesn't care   b. is concerned   c. knows
4. They're *like* family.
   a. enjoyable   b. similar to   c. likable
5. Mr. Chin is a very important *force* in redevelopment.
   a. power   b. developer   c. buyer
6. His company rebuilt the old factory area—a *forgotten* section of town.
   a. revitalized   b. important   c. abandoned
7. The *value* of the building will increase after reconstruction.
   a. size   b. worth   c. shape

D REACT

Work on your own. *Complete the following sentences based on the information in the timed reading.*

There are two points of view in this reading.

1. Mr. Harley wants to . . . .

   Mr. Harley is worried because . . . .

2. Mr. Chin wants to . . . .

   Mr. Chin thinks that the old neighborhood and its residents . . . .

What is your point of view?

   Mr. Harley should . . . .

   Mr. Chin should . . . .

   The Johnsons should . . . .

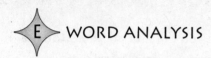

WORD ANALYSIS

PART 1

Read the following information about verbs. Then decide if the italicized words in the sentences are nouns or verbs.

A **verb** expresses action (*walk, talk*) or relation (*be, seem*) involving other words. Every sentence has a verb.

	NOUN	VERB
1. Political attitudes often *shift* from left to right.	____	____
2. In the 1960s, there was a sharp *increase* in crime.	____	____
3. What kind of *change* are you talking about?	____	____
4. The population *shift* to the Sun Belt occurred in the 1970s.	____	____
5. At that time, population *increased* in the South but decreased in the North.	____	____
6. *Progress* in this kind of weather is impossible.	____	____
7. Mobility means that people *move* from one situation to another.	____	____
8. The members reported little *progress* in the talks.	____	____
9. Don't make a *move*!	____	____
10. It sometimes seems that things *change* slowly.	____	____

PART 2

1. Study the meaning of these: Can you think of another example?

re-	again	**re**build	_____
		revitalize	
		reapply	
		review	
bene-	good	**bene**fit	_____
		beneficial	
com-	together	**com**munity	_____
		committee	
con-		**con**vention	
ven-	come	con**ven**tion	_____
		in**ven**t	

2. Complete the sentences with one of the above words.

   a. We don't have classes today because all the teachers went to a

   _____.

   b. After the earthquake, they had to _____ the city.

   c. I have to _____ the vocabulary before the test.

   d. An additional _____ of living in the city is good schools.

   e. The president asked a _____ of seven people to study the
      problem and report back to him.

   f. Our neighborhood has a real sense of _____. We often have

      parties together, and we cooperate on a lot of different projects.

   g. The university didn't accept me, but I'm going to _____ next
      year.

LOOK BACK

 VOCABULARY

Circle the letter of the choice that best completes each sentence.

1. She is very kind to all the people who live on her street. She is very __.
   a. neighborly   b. wealthy   c. reflective

2. I live in a __ area. I take the bus to the city, and I get to the office in twenty minutes.
   a. revitalized   b. social   c. suburban

3. Yesterday I found an old table in my grandmother's house. It is old, but with some __, it will be beautiful.
   a. employment   b. restoration   c. opportunity

4. We do not agree. We can't decide. Our ideas are __.
   a. entertaining   b. conflicting   c. expanding

5. Condominiums are __ for some city residents.
   a. mobile   b. rebuilding   c. beneficial

6. You must __ productivity to earn money.
   a. decrease   b. contain   c. increase

7. He is a peaceful man. He doesn't like __.
   a. entertainment   b. violence   c. opportunity

8. That movie is not good for children. It's a(n) __ movie.
   a. modern   b. prosperous   c. adult

9. That apartment has many large rooms; it's very __.
   a. residential   b. excitable   c. spacious

10. Poverty and __ are negative aspects of modern city life.
    a. prosperity   b. violence   c. similarity

MATCHING

Find the word or phrase in column B that has a similar meaning to a word or phrase in column A. Write the letter of that word or phrase next to the word in column A.

	A		B
1. _____	reflect	a.	prosperous
2. _____	wealthy	b.	many
3. _____	area of residences	c.	mirror
4. _____	people who live in a place	d.	revitalize
5. _____	countless	e.	part
6. _____	similar to	f.	grow smaller
7. _____	decrease	g.	population
8. _____	problem	h.	have within
9. _____	rebuild	i.	conflict
10. _____	number of people	j.	residents
11. _____	aspect	k.	neighborhood
12. _____	opportunities	l.	like
13. _____	increase	m.	grow larger
14. _____	benefit	n.	advantage
15. _____	contain	o.	chances

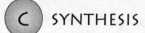

C SYNTHESIS

Work together. *Read the following group projects. Choose one to investigate.*

1. **Plan a trip** to a particular city you would like to visit. Go to a travel agency to get brochures about the city and/or write a short letter asking for information to the city hall, the mayor's office, or the Chamber of Commerce of the city you would like to visit. Where can you stay? What can you see? Are there special sections of the city that are interesting? How can you get around the city? Are there famous places to see?

2. **Look at housing in your area.** Use the local newspaper to see what kind of housing there is in your area. Is it expensive to rent an apartment? Are there condominiums in your area? One-family houses? How do the prices compare in different neighborhoods?

3. **Choose a city.** Your company wants to give you a better job. You can choose to work in their offices in Miami, Chicago, or Seattle. What are the advantages and disadvantages of living in each city? Which one would you choose? Why?

Share the information that your group finds with the whole class.

D VOCABULARY PREVIEW

What shorter words can you see in these words from Chapter 4?

1. popularity   _popular_

2. addition   _____

3. unhealthy   _____

4. unchanging   _____

5. international   _____

6. mixture   _____

7. rediscovering   _____

8. What words have a prefix that means not? _____

4 FOOD IN AMERICA

A FIRST LOOK

A BACKGROUND BUILDING

Work on your own. *Wherever you come from, food is an important part of life. Think about your day yesterday, and answer the following questions.*

1. Did you eat breakfast?   Yes   No

   Alone?   With family?   With friends?

2. If yes, what did you have?

   Drinks: coffee, tea, milk, juice

   Food: toast, cereal, eggs, pancakes, doughnuts

3. Did you eat lunch?   Yes   No

   Alone?   With family?   With friends?

4. What did you have?

5. Did you eat dinner in a restaurant?   In a cafeteria?   At home?

   Alone?   With family?   With friends?

6. What did you have?

7. If you ate at home, who cooked?

Work together. *Share your answers with a partner.*

TOPIC

Before you begin to read, look at these topics. There is one topic for each paragraph. Look quickly at the reading to find these topics. Do not read every word at this point. Write the number of the paragraph next to the topic of that paragraph.

1. _____ fast food

2. _____ ethnic food

3. _____ traditional food in the United States

4. _____ a return to natural, unprocessed food

5. _____ changing attitudes about food

C READING

Now read.

FOOD IN AMERICA

1   Many changes are taking place in "food styles" in the United States. The United States is traditionally famous for its very solid and unchanging diet of meat and potatoes. Now we have many different alternatives to choose from: various ethnic food, health food, and fast food, in addition to the traditional home-cooked meal.

2   Ethnic restaurants and supermarkets are commonplace in the United States. Because the United States is a country of immigrants, there is an immense variety. Any large American city is filled with restaurants serving international cooking. Many cities even have ethnic sections: Chinatown, Little Italy, or Germantown. With this vast ethnic choice, we can enjoy food from all over the world. This is pleasant for those who come here to travel or to work; they can usually find their native specialties: *tabouli, arepas,* or *miso* soup. Besides sections of the cities, there are regions that are well known for certain food because of the people who settled there. For example, southern California has many Mexican restaurants, and Louisiana has a strong Creole accent to its food. (Creole is a mixture of French, African, and Caribbean Island food.)

3   Health food gained popularity when people began to think more seriously about their physical well-being. Health food is fresh, natural, unprocessed food. It does not contain preservatives to make it last longer or chemicals to make it taste or look better. Some health food enthusiasts are vegetarians: They eat no meat; they prefer to get their essential proteins from other sources, such as beans and rice, cheese, and eggs. More and more people are eating healthy food and trying to eat less fat and red meat.

4   Fast-food restaurants continue to expand rapidly all over the country. In the United States, speed at lunchtime is a very important factor. People usually have a short lunch break, or they just do not want to waste their time eating. Fast-food restaurants are places that take care of hundreds of people in a short time. There is usually very little waiting, and the food is usually cheap. Some examples are 'burger and pizza places.

5   America's attitude toward meals is changing, too. The traditional big breakfast and dinner at 6:00 P.M. are losing popularity. People are rediscovering the social importance of food. Dinner with family or friends is again becoming a very special way of enjoying and sharing. Like so many people in other cultures, many Americans are taking time to relax and enjoy the finer tastes at dinner, even if they still rush through lunch at a hamburger stand.

REACT

Underline one idea which surprised you in the reading. Tell a partner why it surprised you.

D SCANNING/VOCABULARY

PART 1

*Scan the reading for these words. Write the number of the line where you find the word. Then compare its meaning in the sentence to the meaning of the word(s) on the right. Are the words similar or different? Write **similar** or **different** on the line.*

		LINE NUMBER		SIMILAR OR DIFFERENT?
1.	traditionally	____	recently	____
2.	waste	____	use with no benefit	____
3.	essential	____	important	____
4.	unchanging	____	fixed	____
5.	native	____	foreign	____
6.	gained	____	increased	____
7.	well-being	____	health	____
8.	fresh	____	processed	____
9.	vegetarian	____	meat-eater	____
10.	taking time	____	rush	____

PART 2

Find a word or words in the reading that has (or have) the same meaning as the word(s) below, and write it on the line. The number of the line is given to help you.

1.	Line 2	well-known	____
2.	Line 3	choices	____
3.	Line 4	different	____
4.	Line 6	usual	____
5.	Line 6	cultural	____
6.	Line 9	areas	____
7.	Line 11	enjoyable	____
8.	Line 21	important	____
9.	Line 28	inexpensive	____
10.	Line 30	feeling	____

READING COMPREHENSION

Answer the following questions about each of the paragraphs in the reading.

Paragraph 1. Three categories of food are:

a. _____

b. _____

c. _____

Paragraph 2. In the United States, there is food from around the world. Give two examples:

a. _____

b. _____

Paragraph 3. Many people are now interested in health food. What is

health food? _____

Paragraph 4. Fast food has become very popular. Write two reasons why.

a. _____

b. _____

Paragraph 5. Americans are changing their feelings about food. Write two examples of how.

a. They _____

b. They _____

LOOK AGAIN

 A VOCABULARY

Circle the letter of the choice that best completes each sentence.

1. She is always on television. She is a(n) __ newscaster.

   a. traditional   b. essential   c. well-known

2. Fast-food restaurants are now __.

   a. specialties   b. commonplace   c. factors

3. Immigration is an important factor in the __ of ethnic restaurants.

   a. sharing   b. source   c. popularity

4. I like to prepare food ahead of time because I hate to __ when I make dinner for guests.

   a. rush   b. choose   c. relax

5. It is __ to have protein.

   a. traditional   b. ethnic   c. essential

6. Many people __ energy; they use it without thinking.

   a. waste   b. rush   c. rediscover

7. Those restaurants are very popular here. Now they are __ into different areas of the country.

   a. growing   b. expanding   c. rushing

8. Don't buy that bread. It isn't __.

   a. possible   b. fresh   c. processed

9. Meat is a __ of protein.

   a. factor   b. taste   c. source

10. American Indians are __ Americans.

   a. native   b. foreign   c. international

READING COMPREHENSION

Circle the letter of the choice that best completes each sentence.

1. Meat and potatoes are examples of __.

   a. the traditional American diet   b. processed food   c. health

2. Speed is a factor in the popularity of __.

   a. our attitude   b. lunch breaks   c. fast-food restaurants

3. Germantown is an example of __.

   a. international cooking   b. an ethnic neighborhood   c. a regional specialty

4. The author thinks that Americans are now eating dinner __.

   a. at 6:00 P.M.   b. more slowly   c. later

5. Health food enthusiasts often __.

   a. like meat   b. are vegetarians   c. eat processed food

6. People who come to the United States are pleased because __.

   a. they can find their native food   b. there are many regional specialties   c. American food is traditional

7. Americans are relaxing at dinner, but they are still __.

   a. rushing at lunch   b. sharing it   c. losing popularity

8. Two important factors in fast-food restaurants are __.

   a. speed and cost   b. expansions and lunch breaks   c. 'burger and pizza places

9. __ is a source of protein.

   a. Fruit   b. Meat   c. Natural food

10. An example of the traditional American attitude toward food is __.

    a. a late lunch   b. a quick lunch   c. health food

C THINK ABOUT IT

Work on your own. *Answer the following questions.*

1. What are the most popular dishes in your country?

2. Is there fast food in your country? What is it like?

3. Which kind of food is eaten most often in your country? Beef? Fish? Chicken?

Work together. Share your ideas with a partner.

D GRAPH READING

PART 1

What do Americans eat?

Read the graph on the right (Figure 5), and answer the following questions.

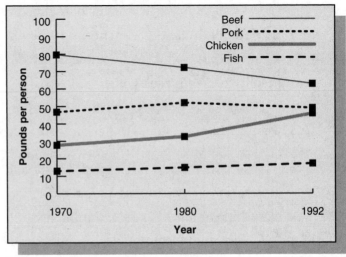

Source: U. S. Department of Agriculture

FIGURE 5

1. This graph shows changes in American eating style. What four foods are

   listed? _____ _____ _____ _____

2. According to the graph, which of the four is the most popular in the

   United States?

   _____

3. Which is the least popular? _____

4. Which of the four increased most in popularity? _____

5. Name one piece of information from the graph that surprised you.

   _____

6. Would the graph be different for people from your country? If not, why

   not? If yes, why? _____

PART 2

What do Americans drink?

Label the graph in Figure 6 according to the reading.

In the year 1992, *soft drinks* such as colas were the most popular drinks in the United States, consumed at the rate of 44 gallons per person per year. *Coffee* was the next most popular drink at 28 gallons per person, followed by *milk* at 25 gallons. Bottled water was at just over 8 gallons, and *tea* was at 7 gallons, quite a bit below coffee. *Juice* was at almost 7 gallons. As for alcoholic drinks, *beer* was at 33 gallons per person. *Wine* was only slightly higher (2.7 gallons) than *other alcoholic drinks* (whiskey, vodka, etc.), which were the least popular of all drinks at 2 gallons per person.

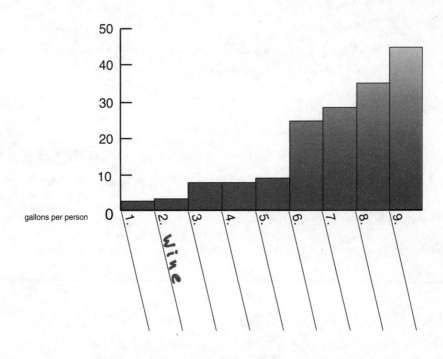

FIGURE 6

CONTACT A POINT OF VIEW

 BACKGROUND BUILDING

Popcorn, potato chips, and candy are favorite foods for lots of Americans.
Food such as this, which does not have nutritional value for the body, is
often called *junk food*—meaning worthless or without any value. Think
about what you have eaten during the last 24 hours. Did you have any junk
food?

B TIMED READING

Read the following point of view, and answer the questions in four minutes.

All right! enough cookies, cola, and chips! It seems that junk food is all that children want to eat these days. Television controls their tastes. The kids see well-known personalities eating potato chips, candy, and other processed food, and they want to be like their heroes. How do they do it? They eat the same food. I wish there were more characters like old Popeye the sailor, who ate spinach and not french fries.

Just because I like brown rice, beans, and fresh vegetables, I don't expect my children to eat this "health food." I'm glad to cook traditional meals of meat and potatoes for them. I really can't be too upset with the kids because most adults aren't careful about what they eat. The other night, my wife and I went to a party where there was plenty to drink but very little for us to eat. They served hot dogs and hamburgers. I can't eat hot dogs, with all those preservatives, and hamburgers are filled with chemicals so that they look good. Besides the meat, they had sugar-filled cookies and cake, and, of course, chips. Terrible! I don't want the world to change because of me, but I think that people should realize that there are alternatives to eating meat. They always tell me that I probably don't get my essential proteins. But I feel better than ever, and I'm sure that it's because I'm vegetarian. I would really like to see more television advertisements that show the benefits of good, healthy, natural food.

Read the following statements carefully to determine whether each is true (T), false (F), or impossible to know (ITK).

1. _____ Cookies and chips are junk food.

2. _____ The author feels very healthy.

3. _____ Brown rice is junk food.

4. _____ Children want to eat junk food.

5. _____ The author eats meat.

6. _____ The author is married.

7. _____ Television influences children's food choices.

8. _____ Popeye ate only junk food.

9. _____ There are many TV advertisements for health food.

10. _____ If necessary, the author will serve meat and potatoes to the kids.

C VOCABULARY

Choose one of the vocabulary words from the timed reading, and fill in the blanks in these sentences. Make necessary changes in the form of the word.

1. processed/junk/taste/spinach

   _____ is not _____ food; it _____ good

   because it is not _____ or treated with chemicals.

2. essential/careful/enough/plenty

   People should be _____ about getting _____ of

   _____ proteins. Many people do not get _____.

3. fresh/expect/upset

   She was _____ at the restaurant because she _____ to

   get _____ vegetables, not canned ones.

4. personalities/heroes/influence

   Many children's _____ are TV _____. These people

   often _____ the attitudes of the children.

D REACT

America's attitude toward food is different from many other countries. Have you changed your "food style" in the United States? Put a check beside the following statements that are true for you. Share your ideas with a classmate or with the class.

In the United States, I eat

_____ more food	_____ less food
_____ more meat	_____ less meat
_____ more junk food	_____ less fresh food
_____ more frozen food	_____ fewer sweets
_____ more canned food	
_____ more at breakfast	_____ less at breakfast
_____ more at lunch	_____ less at lunch
_____ more at dinner	_____ less at dinner
_____ a faster breakfast	_____ a later breakfast
_____ in restaurants more often	_____ a later dinner
_____ more often	_____ less often

In the United States, I ate some things for the first time.

I really like _____.

I really hate _____.

WORD ANALYSIS

PART 1

*Look at the endings for **adjectives** below. Are the italicized words in the sentences adjectives or nouns?*

	NOUNS	ADJECTIVES
-ful	success	success**ful** (full of)
-less	value	value**less** (without)
-ous	religion	religi**ous**

Note that *-ful* and *-less* cannot be added to all nouns. For example, *valueful* is not a word, but *valueless* is.

	NOUNS	ADJECTIVES
1. His work is always *careless* and messy.	___	___
2. That's a *wonderful* idea.	___	___
3. A *thoughtful* person is one who is kind.	___	___
4. There are *various* possibilities for the party.	___	___
5. Everyone was shocked. It was a *senseless* murder.	___	___
6. He does everything with *care*.	___	___
7. How important is *success*?	___	___
8. Only a few things in life are *changeless*.	___	___
9. That diamond is a *priceless* antique.	___	___
10. She watched the kitten with *wonder*.	___	___

PART 2

In other chapters, you have studied the parts of the boldfaced words in the following sentences. On the line, write the letter of the meaning of the word from the list below.

1. Street noise is one of the **disadvantages** of living in the city. _h_

2. Many people have gone to a university on the scholarships your company established, so the **benevolence** of your company is well-known. ___

3. The milk in this country is **homogenized**. ___

4. Some universities in the United States have **coeducational** dormitories. ___

5. Studies show that smoking cigarettes is **unhealthy**. ___

6. The union disagreed with parts of the contract, so the union and the company will have to **renegotiate** the contract. ___

7. All the scientists **convened** at a meeting in Geneva. ___

8. The **community** ___ is quite **heterogeneous** ___ so my children are learning to accept different customs and values.

9. The children **dislike** ___ each other, but they usually **cooperate** ___ with me.

a. negotiate again

b. came together

c. group of people living in the same area

d. do not like

e. wish to do good

f. different from each other

g. mixed well

h. bad things, not an advantage

i. not healthy

j. work together well

k. male and female students together

LOOK BACK

 VOCABULARY

Circle the letter of the choice that best completes each sentence.

1. He is a strong, __ candidate for the presidency.
   a. commonplace   b. solid   c. rushed

2. Using a lot of electricity is __.
   a. rediscovering   b. wasteful   c. well known

3. The Pacific Ocean is very __.
   a. processed   b. expansive   c. gaining

4. The food is inexpensive but __.
   a. tasty   b. social   c. structured

5. He dislikes everything; he has a very poor __.
   a. well-being   b. popularity   c. attitude

6. There are __ immigrant groups in most large American cities.
   a. various   b. unchanging   c. popular

7. What kind of __ does that pie have?
   a. filling   b. importance   c. pleasantness

8. __ is important in fish.
   a. Control   b. Freshness   c. Diet

9. __ is an important factor for most movie personalities.
   a. Fame   b. Gain   c. Tradition

10. The __ of life is a question for all human beings. What is life's meaning?
    a. waste   b. essence   c. attitude

B MATCHING

Find the word in column B that has a similar meaning to a word in column A.
Write the letter of that word next to the word in column A

	A		B
1. ____	upset	a.	important
2. ____	essential	b.	use poorly
3. ____	diet	c.	rush
4. ____	minimal	d.	worried
5. ____	immense	e.	large
6. ____	waste	f.	choice of food
7. ____	alternative	g.	well known
8. ____	famous	h.	grow
9. ____	hurry	i.	plenty
10. ____	expand	j.	commonplace
11. ____	usual	k.	choice
12. ____	a lot	l.	almost none

 C SYNTHESIS

Work together.

1. If you are living in another country, what kind of food do you miss most from home? If you could have any dish from home right now, what would it be?

2. Many people say that they really like ice cream in the United States. Do you have a favorite American dish?

3. Make a directory of restaurants near your school for new students. Include information about the type of food, the atmosphere (formal or informal), and the price.

D VOCABULARY PREVIEW

What shorter words can you see in these words from Chapter 5?

1. specialist _____
2. unlucky _____
3. unfamiliar _____
4. newcomers _____
5. friendliness _____
6. intercultural _____
7. knowledge _____

8. unreality _____
9. familiarity _____
10. successful _____
11. impression _____
12. disoriented _____
13. homesick _____
14. illness _____

15. international, intercultural: *inter* means _____

Another example: _____

16. self-conscious, self-image: *self* means _____

Another example: _____

E SKIMMING

Look quickly at the next page. Answer these questions.

1. What is this page?
2. How is it organized?

F SCANNING

Answer these questions as quickly as possible.

1. How many different kinds of restaurants are listed here?
2. What is the name of an Indonesian restaurant?
3. Which restaurants recommend reservations?
4. Where is Zola located?
5. How many Japanese restaurants are there?
6. Which restaurants are open after midnight?
7. Which restaurant serves Kirin beer?
8. How many health food restaurants are listed?
9. Is Assad's an Indian restaurant?
10. Where would you like to eat tonight?

RESTAURANTS
A guide arranged by cuisine

Chinese

BEIJING 200 Center St. 555-5877
DRAGON INN 15 Pleasant. 555-1134
POLYNESIAN VILLAGE
   Chinese and Polynesian Cuisine
   Luncheon Specials
   209 Sidney Ave 555-6892
WOK AWAY 54 Spring 555-9987

Fast Food

BURGER AND COKE
   15 Roosevelt Ave 555-7896
SAL'S SUBS
   Best Subs in Town!
   2326 Michigan Dr 555-8777
PIZZA PARLOR
   Open Until 3:00 AM
   654 Doolittle St. 555-4837

French

AUTRE MOMENT
   Recommended by CITY MAGAZINE
   Function Room Private Parties
   1 Bedford Place 555-1674
BRASSERIE FRANÇAIS 13 Dresser St. . . . 555-1667
CHEZ FRANCINE
   Elegant Dining Thurs - Sat
   Reservations Recommended
   28 Simon St. 555-1562
LE SANDWICH 2 Cook St. 555-9981
ZOLA 5 Pinyon Place 555-1943

German

HAUFBRAU 1779 Dwight Ave 555-1329

Greek

ACROPOLIS
   Lunch and DInner
   11:00 AM to Midnight
   A Taste of the Greek Islands
   653 Fourth Ave 555-5968

Health Food

ALICE'S KITCHEN
   Near Uptown Shopping Center
   23 Arlington 555-1563

NATURAL NUTRITION 1225 East 3rd 555-1967
WHOLE EARTH EATERY
   All Natural Ingredients
   Open for Lunch and Dinner
   9 Knox St. 555-1647

Indian

CURRY PALACE
   1276 Fourth St. Old Town 555-6719
TAJ MAHAL
   India at Its Best
   3390 New London St 555-8030
TASTE OF INDIA 4 Madison Park 555-1378
ROYAL INDIA
   Open Until 1:30 AM
   7890 Hirsch 555-1984

Indonesian

JAKARTA RESTAURANT Park Ave 555-6767

Japanese

KYOTO RESTAURANT
   Sushi/Sashimi/Kirin Beer
   3447 Elliot Ave. 555-1456
SAMURAI 14 New Britton St 555-1457
GEISHA INN
   Call For Reservations
   13 Squire Rd 555-3546
MIKA 5659 Cutler Ave 555-1545
TEMPURA 4897 King SW 555-8767
HANA RESTAURANT 11402 18th St 555-1223

Mexican

CASA LOPEZ
   433 Drummer Blvd. Sea Town 555-5645
THE CHILE FACTORY
   Best Salsa in Town
   850 Marion Way 555-6778
PACO'S 18 Dwight 555-4545
TORTILLA EXPRESS
   Johnson Ave at Milbrook 555-5867

Middle East

FALAFAL 455 Bruce Dr. 555-6778
ASSAD'S 19987 Spring Valley Parkway. . . . 555-3467
SAID'S SANDWICHES 1675 Murdock St. . 555-4545

FIGURE 7

5 CULTURE SHOCK

A FIRST LOOK

 BACKGROUND BUILDING

Work on your own. *Answer these questions about yourself. The ones on this page are about your first days in the U.S. The ones on the next page are about how you feel now.*

My First Days in the U.S.

I _____ life in America.

    a. loved   b. hated   c. had no strong feelings about

I _____ being with Americans.

    a. loved   b. hated   c. had no strong feelings about

I _____ English.

    a. loved   b. hated   c. had no strong feelings about

I _____ homesick most of the time.

    a. was not   b. was

I wanted to spend my time with _____.

    a. Americans   b. people from my culture

I wanted to speak _____.

    a. English   b. my language

I thought life in America was _____.

    a. wonderful   b. terrible

I thought Americans were _____.

    a. wonderful   b. terrible

I _____ to go home after one week.

    a. didn't want   b. wanted

Count your "a" answers and your "b" answers.   a. _____   b. _____

Now

I _____ life in America.

    a. love   b. hate   c. have no strong feelings about

I _____ being with Americans.

    a. love   b. hate   c. have no strong feelings about

I _____ English.

    a. love   b. hate   c. have no strong feelings about

I _____ homesick most of the time.

    a. am not   b. am

I want to spend my time with _____.

    a. Americans   b. people from my culture

I want to speak _____.

    a. English   b. my language

I think life in America is _____.

    a. wonderful   b. terrible

I think Americans are _____.

    a. wonderful   b. terrible

I _____ to go home in one week.

    a. don't want   b. want

Count your "a" answers and your "b" answers.   a. _____   b. _____

The title of this chapter is "Culture Shock." What do you think that means?

B   TOPIC

Before you begin to read, look at these topics. There is one topic for each paragraph. Look quickly at the reading to find these topics. Do not read every word at this point. Write the number of the paragraph next to the topic of that paragraph.

1. _____   the people who experience culture shock

2. _____   the things people say when you leave home

3. _____   three stages of culture shock

4. _____   the feelings of culture shock

5. _____   problems in a new culture

6. _____   definition of culture shock

C   READING

Now read.

CULTURE SHOCK

1   "You're going to the United States to live? How wonderful! You're really
lucky!"

2   Does this sound familiar? Perhaps your family and friends said similar things
to you when you left home. But does it seem true all the time? Is your life in this
new country always wonderful and exciting? Specialists in counseling and
intercultural studies say that it is not easy to adjust to life in a new culture. They
call the feelings that people experience when they come to a new environment
culture shock.

3   According to these specialists, there are three stages of culture shock. In
the first stage, the newcomers like their environment. Then, when the newness
wears off, they begin to hate the city, the country, the people, the apartment,
and everything else in the new culture. In the final stage of culture shock, the
newcomers begin to adjust to their surroundings and, as a result, enjoy their life
more.

4   Some of the reasons for culture shock are obvious. Maybe the weather is
unpleasant. Perhaps the customs are different. Perhaps the public service
systems such as the telephone, post office, or transportation are difficult to
figure out, and you make mistakes. The simplest things seem difficult. The
language may be difficult. How many times have you just repeated the same thing
again and again and hoped to understand the answer eventually? The food may
seem strange to you, and you may miss the familiar smells of the food you are
accustomed to in your own country. If you don't look similar to the natives, you
may feel strange. You may feel like everyone is watching you. In fact, you are
always watching yourself. You are self-conscious.

5   Who experiences culture shock? Everyone does in some form or another.
But culture shock comes as a surprise to most people. A lot of the time, the
people with the worst culture shock are the people who never had any
difficulties in their own countries. They were active and successful in their
community. They had hobbies or pastimes that they enjoyed. When they come
to a new country, they do not have the same established positions or hobbies.
They find themselves without a role, almost without an identity. They have to
build a new self-image.

6   Culture shock produces a feeling of disorientation. This disorientation may
be homesickness, imagined illness, or even paranoia (unreasonable fear). When
people feel the disorientation of culture shock, they sometimes feel like staying
inside all the time. They want to protect themselves from the unfamiliar
environment. They want to create an escape within their room or apartment to
give themselves a sense of security. This escape does solve the problem of
culture shock for the short term, but it does nothing to familiarize the person
more with the culture. Familiarity and experience are the long-term solutions to
the problem of culture shock.

REACT

1. Look at the reading. Underline a sentence you agree with.

2. Underline a sentence you don't understand.

3. Discuss these sentences with your classmates and teacher.

 ## SCANNING/VOCABULARY

PART 1

Write the line number where you find the word(s). Then circle the letter of the choice with the best meaning for the word as it is used in that sentence.

1. specialists   line number __

   a. experts   b. important people   c. doctors

2. environment   line number __

   a. place around you   b. time you live in   c. country

3. stages   line number __

   a. part of a theater   b. levels   c. transportation

4. final   line number __

   a. most important   b. most difficult   c. last

5. obvious   line number __

   a. easy to see   b. difficult   c. different

6. figure out   line number __

   a. see   b. design   c. understand

7. self-conscious   line number __

   a. aware of yourself   b. embarrassed   c. homesick

8. role   line number __

   a. part in a play   b. friend   c. position

9. paranoia   line number __

   a. good feeling   b. imagined illness   c. unreasonable fear

10. term   line number __

    a. condition   b. word or expression   c. length of time

PART 2

Find a word that is the opposite of the one given. The line where you will find the word is given.

1. line 2   unlucky   _____

2. line 10   natives   _____

3. line 18   most difficult _____

4. line 21   forget   _____

5. line 27   best   _____

6. line 28   lazy   _____

7. line 34   real   _____

8. line 37   destroy   _____

E READING COMPREHENSION

Circle the letter of the choice that best completes each sentence.

1. There are apparently __ stages of culture shock.

   a. two   b. three   c. four

2. People who come to a new environment __ feel lucky and happy.

   a. do not always   b. always   c. never

3. According to the author, it __ easy to adjust to a new culture.

   a. is always   b. is usually   c. is not

4. The author gives __ examples of public service systems.

   a. two   b. three   c. four

5. Someone who looks __ the natives of a country may feel strange.

   a. similar to   b. at   c. different from

6. People in a foreign culture feel __ about themselves and their positions.

   a. differently   b. the same   c. happy

7. The author gives __ examples of the disorientation of culture shock.

   a. two   b. three   c. four

8. The author thinks that it is __ idea for people feeling culture shock to stay in their homes as a long-term solution to culture shock.

   a. not a good   b. a great   c. not a bad

9. In the final stage of culture shock, people __ the new environment.

   a. love   b. adjust to   c. hate

10. People who feel culture shock stay at home because of __.

    a. insecurity   b. solutions   c. the weather

LOOK AGAIN

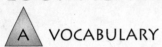

A VOCABULARY

Circle the letter of the choice that best completes each sentence.

1. In this reading, a specialist is probably __.

   a. a doctor   b. an authority   c. a newcomer

2. Your __ is the area around you.

   a. environment   b. culture   c. self-image

3. Disorientation is a feeling of __.

   a. security   b. knowledge   c. unreality

4. I can't figure out my homework. I can't __ it.

   a. remember   b. escape from   c. understand

5. I am bored. My life is not __ enough.

   a. experienced   b. active   c. essential

6. People usually have hobbies for __.

   a. money   b. enjoyment   c. a job

7. A newcomer is __ the area around him or her.

   a. unfamiliar with   b. unhappy about   c. accustomed to

8. When you feel that everyone is watching you, you are __.

   a. secure   b. self-conscious   c. unfamiliar

9. Paranoia is a feeling of __.

   a. fear   b. happiness   c. experience

10. I don't know him. I don't know his __.

   a. system   b. identity   c. term

B READING COMPREHENSION

Complete the reading summary with words from this list. Try to complete it first without looking back at the reading.

adjusting	hating	shock
culture	liking	short-term
different	long-term	solution
experience	problems	sometimes
familiarity		

Adjusting to a new (1) _____ is not easy. The experience of (2) _____ to a new environment is called culture (3) _____. There are three stages of culture shock: (4) _____ the new environment, (5) _____ it, and adjusting to it. People experience culture shock because of (6) _____ customs, weather, and food and because of language (7) _____. (8) _____ the people with the worst culture shock are people who never had any difficulties in their own country. The (9) _____ (10) _____ to culture shock is to stay at home and try to escape. The (11) _____ solutions are (12) _____ and (13) _____.

C THINK ABOUT IT

Discuss the answers to these questions with your classmates.

1. What was your favorite hobby or pastime when you were in your country? Is it possible to enjoy those things in the United States?

2. Is there any activity that you enjoy (or might enjoy) doing in your free time in the United States? What is that? How difficult or expensive is it to do?

3. Do you feel safe and confident about going out in your new environment? Do you enjoy finding new things to do and new places to visit?

D READING

Read the following paragraph, and answer the questions below.

Jody and her family spent a year in England while her husband was in a graduate program there. They lived in a friendly community and traveled to a lot of interesting places in the U.K. and in Europe. Back at home in the United States, Jody told her friends about their wonderful year. She said that England was a great place to spend a year, even though she wouldn't want to live there permanently. Jody was happy to be home, but she felt strange. Even one month after her trip, she didn't have any energy and kept doing stupid things—she left her wallet at stores twice, forgot to meet people for lunch, and forgot to keep other appointments. She didn't feel like cooking, and she spent a lot of time sleeping.

1. Where is Jody's home?

2. Did she have a good time during her year in England? Why or why not?

3. What do you think was the problem for Jody when she came back home? (answer below)

4. What can Jody do to feel better? (answer below)

Answer to 3: Jody was suffering from the *fourth* stage of culture shock—the readjustment people have when they return to their countries.

Answer to 4: Jody will feel better after a while. She needs time to put her trip into perspective and adjust to her normal life in the United States.

CONTACT A POINT OF VIEW

 A **BACKGROUND BUILDING**

1. What do you think the above illustration means?

2. Do you ever feel like the person in the illustration? Why or why not?

Read the following point of view, and answer the questions in four minutes.

Nguyen Chau Van Loc came to the United States in 1979 from Vietnam. His first impression of the United States was very positive. He was particularly impressed with the way Americans had put technology to work for them. Americans have machines to take them upstairs and downstairs, give them money at the bank, and even open doors for them. He felt that this new environment offered him many exciting opportunities.

However, Loc quickly found himself unprepared to take advantage of these opportunities. He knew almost no English. Even when he knew what to say on a bus or in a store, no one understood him, and he had to repeat and repeat. In Vietnam, Loc was a technician, but in the United States, he did not have enough experience compared with other people. He had trouble finding a job. He felt that he did not have an important role or position in the city and missed the security and friendliness of his town in Vietnam. He felt that he would never learn English or feel happy in the United States. He began to feel very depressed and homesick.

Loc was lucky because there was a counselor in his English program. This counselor helped Loc to understand that his feelings were normal and that they were only a stage in his adjustment to this new culture. Loc began to look around him and to talk to other Vietnamese. He saw that many others felt the same way he did. Some, in fact, were more disoriented than he was and were afraid to go out into the city.

Eventually, Loc began to feel better about his life in the United States. He developed a position in the Vietnamese American community and adjusted to his new role in American society. He is accustomed to his life in this new country but will always miss Vietnam.

Read the following statements carefully to determine whether each is true (T), false (F), or impossible to know (ITK).

1. _____ Loc came from Vietnam.
2. _____ Loc is married.
3. _____ Loc came to the United States in 1977.
4. _____ Loc had a positive attitude about American technology.
5. _____ Loc did not have a job in Vietnam.
6. _____ A counselor helped Loc.
7. _____ The counselor was a woman.
8. _____ No one felt the same way that Loc did.
9. _____ People understood Loc's English easily.
10. _____ Loc never thinks about Vietnam now.

C VOCABULARY

Circle the letter of the choice with the same meaning as the italicized word(s).

1. My first *impression* of the teacher was good.
   a. experience with   b. conversation with   c. ideas about

2. American *technology* surprised the Vietnamese immigrant.
   a. scientific development   b. machines   c. industry

3. There are many *opportunities* for work in the city.
   a. possibilities   b. difficulties   c. advantages

4. I wrote my homework *again*.
   a. very well   b. another time   c. finally

5. He felt *self-conscious* when he spoke English.
   a. strong   b. tired   c. insecure

6. He was not sure of his *role* in the group.
   a. position   b. friend   c. pay

7. I am always *depressed* on rainy days.
   a. angry   b. tired   c. sad

8. The *counselor* talked to me about my problems.
   a. assistant   b. advisor   c. teacher

9. The newcomers felt *disoriented* in the airport.
   a. mixed up   b. happy   c. homesick

10. The *image* on this television is bad.
    a. picture   b. actor   c. color

D REACT

*When you entered a new environment or culture, what was the most difficult thing you experienced? What was the easiest? Number these things according to the level of difficulty. Write **1** for the hardest and **11** for the easiest. Include all the numbers from **1** to **11**.*

_____ the bank

_____ the transportation system

_____ school

_____ the post office

_____ the living situation (roommates, finding a place to live, neighbors)

_____ making friends

_____ the weather

_____ understanding American customs and lifestyles

_____ understanding American values and beliefs

_____ using the telephone

_____ finding good food to eat

Explain to the other people in your class why you had difficulties with your number 1, the hardest thing. Give examples of your experiences. After you were in this new environment for a while or even now, what was or is the most difficult thing for you? Did the most difficult thing become easier in time, or did it stay the same?

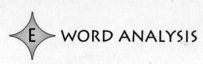

E ► WORD ANALYSIS

PART 1

Look at the endings for nouns and adjectives below. Are the italicized words in the sentences nouns or adjectives? Remember that there is never an -s on the end of an adjective in English.

NOUN		ADJECTIVE	
-ty	socie**ty**	*-ial*	soc**ial**
-tion	tradi**tion**	*-al*	tradition**al**

	NOUN	ADJECTIVE
1. This solution will be *beneficial* for everyone.		✓
2. Our sense of *community* is very important.	✓	
3. *Poverty* is a serious social problem.	✓	
4. *Racial* conflict is an issue in the United States.		✓
5. She is always very *practical*.		✓
6. Downtown is the *central* business area.		✓
7. What is a *typical* name in your country?		✓
8. There is some *similarity* between you and your brother.	✓	
9. Who has *control* here?		✓
10. People in certain countries value *formality* greatly.	✓	

PART 2

1. Study the meanings of these: Can you think of another example?

inter-	between	**inter**cultural **inter**personal	_____
tele-	distance	**tele**vision **tele**scope	_____
vid-, vis-	to see	tele**vi**sion e**vid**ent	_____
phon-	sound	tele**phone** sym**phon**y	_____
self-	oneself	**self**-image **self**less	_____
auto-	self	**auto**graph **auto**matic	_____

2. Complete the sentences with one of the above words.

   a. The ___symphony___ was wonderful. They played Bach and Hayden.

   b. I don't have to change gears in my car. It's an _____.

   c. I am studying to be a psychologist so ___interpersonal___
      communication is very important for me to learn about.

   d. He never thinks about himself, and he's always giving to other

      people. He is really _____.

   e. Last night was very clear, so I took my ___telescope___ outside and
      looked at the stars.

   f. The damage from the earthquake was immediately ___evident___.
      Buildings fell down and fires began. It was a terrible sight.

   g. I have a friend who collects ___autograph___s of famous people.

   h. He is very intelligent, but he has a negative _____. He
      doesn't feel secure about himself at all.

LOOK BACK

A VOCABULARY

Circle the letter of the choice that best completes each sentence.

1. The man studied in the field for thirty-five years. He is a __ in the field.
   a. counselor   b. newcomer   c. specialist

2. I was certainly surprised when I heard the news. I was __.
   a. shocked   b. bored   c. accustomed to it

3. Childhood is the first __ of a person's life. Or is it the second?
   a. stage   b. image   c. impression

4. I collect stamps. That is my __.
   a. development   b. hobby   c. source

5. My first __ of the airport was terrible.
   a. impression   b. newness   c. alternative

6. Some medicine makes people feel tired and __.
   a. homesick   b. familiar   c. disoriented

7. He was born in Kentucky. He is a __ of Kentucky.
   a. native   b. newcomer   c. term

8. There is a good __ feeling in our neighborhood. We all help each other.
   a. custom   b. self-conscious   c. community

9. I have to find a __ to this problem.
   a. stage   b. custom   c. solution

10. He imagined that people were trying to kill him. He was very __.
    a. successful   b. paranoid   c. established

B MATCHING

Find the word or phrase in column B that has a similar meaning to a word in column A. Write the letter of that word or phrase next to the word in column A.

	A		B
1. _____	image	a.	say again
2. _____	unfamiliar	b.	assistance
3. _____	repeat	c.	easy
4. _____	service	d.	change a little
5. _____	fear	e.	stranger
6. _____	environment	f.	strange
7. _____	newcomer	g.	fright
8. _____	adjust	h.	very sad
9. _____	simple	i.	area around you
10. _____	depressed	j.	picture

C SYNTHESIS

Work together.

Find some students who have visited other countries (your country, if possible). Find out what the most difficult thing they experienced there was. Find out if they experienced culture shock in that country or when they returned to their own country.

D VOCABULARY PREVIEW

What shorter words can you see in these words from Chapter 6?

1. hallway   _____ _____
2. personal   _____
3. interaction   _____
4. reaction   _____
5. lifelong   _____ _____
6. increasingly   _____
7. remarry   _____
8. relationships   _____
9. pressure   _____
10. dependence   _____

6 CONTEMPORARY AMERICAN SOCIETY

A FIRST LOOK

 BACKGROUND BUILDING

Work together.

1. Is the illustration on the preceding page surprising to you? Why?

2. What does this illustration suggest to you about the American family?

Work on your own.

1. Complete these sentences about your hometown. You may have more than one answer.

    a. I come from __.

        a. a town   b. a small city   c. a large city

    b. My family has lived there for __.

        a. less than five years b. my whole life   c. many generations

    c. Most of the people in my town/city know me __.

        a. very well   b. a little   c. not well at all

    d. On the street, in my city/town, I say hello to most of the people I see.

        a. yes   b. no

    e. For entertainment, most people in my town/city __.

        a. stay in town   b. go to another town or city

2. Complete these sentences about life in your country.

    a. Divorce is __ in my country.

        a. common   b. fairly common   c. uncommon

    b. Young men and women __ live together before they get married.

        a. often   b. sometimes   c. never

    c. Parents __ want their children to be independent.

        a. do   b. don't

3. What is a question you have about American society? Write it here.

Find the answer by reading this chapter and asking your teacher and other people.

TOPIC

Before you begin to read, look at these topics. There is one topic for each paragraph. Look quickly at the reading to find these topics. Do not read every word at this point. Write the number of the paragraph next to the topic of that paragraph.

1. _____ a society where people move a lot

2. _____ marriage and divorce

3. _____ life for young people now

4. _____ traditional life in a small town

5. _____ bringing up children

C READING

Now read.

CONTEMPORARY AMERICAN SOCIETY

1   In the past fifty years, American society has changed a great deal. Fifty years ago, most Americans lived in small communities. They rarely moved from one area to another, and they usually knew their neighbors at least by name if not by close, personal interaction. Life was so personal in those days that people often joked about it. They said that a person could not even stay home from church on Sunday without the whole town knowing about it. It was difficult to have privacy in a small community like that, but there was usually a sense of security, of belonging, and of community togetherness in such places. Except for church and the local movie theater, there was not much in the way of entertainment. Some people dreamed about moving to the exciting life of the big cities, but most people were happy to live all their lives in the same community.

2   Today few people experience this type of lifelong social interaction or sense of community togetherness. Contemporary American society is much more transient now; people often move from neighborhood to neighborhood, city to city, and coast to coast. It is rare to find people who have lived all their lives in one community. Because people move so frequently, they do not have a chance to get to know their neighbors. Perhaps this is also why Americans tend to have a more casual attitude about friendships than people from some other cultures; Americans are accustomed to leaving friends and making new friends. In this impersonal society, they have lost the habit of saying hello to people they pass on the streets or in the hallways of their apartment buildings.

3   The American family has also gone through many changes in the past fifty years. Primary among these changes is the current attitude about divorce, the legal end of a marriage. Until the 1960s, divorce was quite uncommon. However, in the next twenty years, the number of divorces increased each year. Now, each year, there is one divorce for every two marriages. With less emphasis on tradition, on religion, and on the economic dependence of women on men (due to the increase in the number of working women), Americans seem less likely to remain in a marriage that has problems. They are not forced by economic, social, or religious pressure to stay married. Partly as a reaction to the high divorce rate, many Americans live together without being married. They feel that it is a good idea to know each other well before they become legally tied. This is particularly common in the more liberal areas of the country—the East and West Coasts and the large cities of the North.

4   Since the 1960s, both the number of single-parent families and the number of mothers who work outside the home have doubled. Obviously, children have greater responsibilities in these nontraditional families. However, bringing up children to be independent has always been a part of the American culture. At an early age, American children learn to do things on their own. They learn to

4 take care of themselves by cleaning their rooms, helping with the dishes and the   41
   laundry, and spending time away from their parents, either in daycare, with a   42
   babysitter, or alone. Older children often do work for other people, such as   43
   babysitting or cutting the grass. Most teenagers try to find summer or after-   44
   school jobs so that they can have their own spending money. While in college,   45
   young people usually work part-time and during summer vacations, they work in   46
   a variety of jobs ranging from construction work to waiting on tables in   47
   restaurants.   48

5   In the past, most young people moved away from home when they finished   49
   high school, either to go to college or to get a job and live with friends. Now,   50
   however, the cost of living is so high that many people under age 25 are moving   51
   back in with their parents. Young people are getting married later now than they   52
   used to: The average age for a woman to get married is about 24, and for a man,   53
   26. Newly married couples often postpone having children while they are   54
   establishing careers. Once they have children, they face difficult decisions about 55
   whether the mother should continue working and, if so, who should care for   56
   the children.   57

REACT

In the reading underline one idea that you think is surprising. Talk to a
partner about this idea.

D SCANNING/VOCABULARY

PART 1

Write the line number where you find the words(s). Then circle the letter of the choice with the best meaning for the word as it is used in that sentence.

1. interaction   line number ___
   a. person-to-person contact   b. greeting   c. reaction

2. belonging   line number ___
   a. being a part of   b. owned   c. missing

3. togetherness   line number ___
   a. feeling close   b. living   c. ownership

4. contemporary   line number ___
   a. person of same age   b. modern   c. ordered by time

5. casual   line number ___
   a. easygoing   b. formal   c. serious

6. primary   line number ___
   a. at an early age   b. basic color   c. of first importance

7. remain   line number ___
   a. stay   b. finish   c. end

8. reaction   line number ___
   a. response   b. reason   c. chemical change

9. teenagers   line number ___
   a. young children   b. students   c. older children

10. face   line number ___
    a. front of a building   b. have in front of them   c. the front of the head

PART 2

Find a word that is the opposite of the one given. The line where you will find the word is given.

1. line 2   often   _rarely_

2. line 8   danger   _security_

3. line 15   staying in one place   _moving_

4. line 21   personal   _impersonal_

5. line 25   common   _rare_

6. line 26   decreased   _increased_

7. line 34   conservative   _liberal_

8. line 38   traditional   _non-traditional_

READING COMPREHENSION

Circle the letter of the choice that best completes each sentence.

1. Fifty years ago, Americans moved around __.
   a. a lot
   b. from one area to another
   c. less than they do now

2. The author states that more mothers work outside the home now in __.
   a. single-parent families
   b. general
   c. two-parent families

3. Single-parent families are __.
   a. always single-parent families
   b. more common now than before
   c. three times as numerous as before

4. In line 38, "nontraditional families" means __.
   a. single-parent families
   b. families with the mother working
   c. both a and b

5. People probably __ went to church when they lived in small communities.
   a. rarely
   b. often
   c. sometimes

6. People today __ live all their lives in one community in the United States.
   a. almost never
   b. usually
   c. almost always

7. The author thinks that Americans and people from other cultures have __ ideas about friendships.
   a. similar
   b. strange
   c. different

8. In paragraph 3, the author mentions __ things that used to make divorce difficult.
   a. three
   b. four
   c. seven

9. Fifty years ago, children __.
   a. had greater responsibilities
   b. were probably independent also
   c. were not very independent

10. When people get married now, they probably __.
    a. have more children
    b. live with his parents
    c. wait to have children

LOOK AGAIN

 A VOCABULARY

Circle the letter of the choice that best completes each sentence.

1. People come and go here all the time. It is really a very __ community.
   a. misleading   b. transient   c. dependent

2. I never have coffee __ sugar.
   a. unless   b. in spite of   c. without

3. Business letters are usually very __.
   a. private   b. impersonal   c. pressured

4. A large salary generally gives people financial __.
   a. security   b. statistics   c. assistance

5. I like that class because the teacher __ grammar rules, and I need to understand grammar more clearly.
   a. interacts   b. postpones   c. emphasizes

6. I don't know them very well. We are just __ friends.
   a. personal   b. casual   c. temporary

7. This magazine is over a year old. The news in it isn't __.
   a. tripled   b. current   c. casual

8. A __ is something I do without thinking. I am accustomed to it.
   a. tradition   b. habit   c. reaction

9. They did not associate with each other. They had little __.
   a. dependence   b. personality   c. interaction

10. There was an emergency so we had to __ our meeting.
    a. postpone   b. establish   c. bring up

B READING COMPREHENSION

Complete the following summary of the reading. Try to answer in your own words without looking back at the reading.

Paragraph 1: Introduction

Fifty years ago, people lived in (1) _____ towns. People

(2) _____ their neighbors well.

Paragraph 2

In contrast, American society is (3) _____ now because

(4) _____ .

Paragraph 3

A major change in American society: (5) _____

Some reasons why divorce is more common: less emphasis on

(6) _____ , (7) _____ , and

(8) _____ dependence of women on men.

As a reaction to high divorce rates, (9) _____

_____ .

Paragraph 4

(10) _____ .

Examples: young children help to clean up and spend time with babysitters; older children and teenagers earn money by working for other people.

Paragraph 5

Young people are moving back home with their parents because

(11) _____ .

They are getting married (12) _____ . They have to make

difficult decisions about having (13) _____ and whether

or not the (14) _____ should work.

C THINK ABOUT IT

Answer the following questions.

1. How do you think community life is different in your culture from community life in the United States?

2. How do you think attitudes about friendships are different in your culture from attitudes in the United States?

3. In the United States, working parents have to find someone to take care of their children while they work. Some daycare possibilities are:

   a. children stay at home and someone comes in to take care of them;

   b. children go to another home where someone takes care of them as well as other children;

   c. children go to a daycare center where professionals take care of them.

   Do people in your country need daycare for their children? Explain why or why not.

4. Why do you think people live together before they are married?

5. Write a composition. Compare society in your country to society in the United States.

D READING

Read the following paragraphs, and answer the questions below.

Jack and May Young work at a factory. Jack works days (7 A.M. to 4 P.M.), but May alternates between the day shift and the night shift (4 P.M. to 1 A.M.). They have been married for thirteen years and have two children, Anna, 9, and Justin, 6. Jack has been very unhappy lately, and he and May often argue. Last month, Jack decided to move out, and last week he asked May for a divorce. May doesn't know for sure, but she thinks that Jack is going to move in with a co-worker, a woman with two young children.

May doesn't want a divorce, so this situation is very difficult for her, but, to make matters worse, Jack says that he wants custody of the children. He knows that May is a good mother, but he thinks that he can take better care of the children because he will be home when they are at home.

1. Is May ever at home when the children are not in school?

2. Does Jack have a girlfriend?

3. Who do you think should have custody of the children? Why?

CONTACT A POINT OF VIEW

 BACKGROUND BUILDING

Answer the following questions.

1. When you were a teenager, how did you spend your free time?

2. Did you spend most of your time at your own house, at friends' houses, or out?

3. Do/Did your parents worry about you?

Read the following point of view and answer the questions in four minutes.

My name is Jun Gueco. My wife and I have two kids. We're having a real problem with our daughter Maria. She used to be wonderful, but now she's impossible! At age 13, she has a boyfriend, and she wants to go out alone with him to movies and to parties. We want her to wait until she's 16 to go out on dates. What's the hurry? She's much too young to have a boyfriend. We also don't want her to go to parties unless we know the family. We take her and pick her up, but we don't want her to go around alone with a boy. What will everyone think of her if she goes around with a boy? She doesn't seem to care about her reputation, but we know how important it is to be a good girl, especially when she's ready to get married. No one will want to marry a girl with a bad reputation.

Of course our daughter thinks *we're* impossible. She says we're completely out of touch and want everything to be the way it was in the Philippines when we were growing up. I ask her, "What's wrong with that?" Why does she have to be so American? There's nothing wrong with our values just because they're different from the way her American friends live. I think children in the United States have too much freedom. In the Philippines, children spend more time with their family, and they obey their parents. That's the way I want my children to behave, too.

Read the following statements carefully to determine whether each is true (T), false (F), or impossible to know (ITK).

1. _____ Jun has two daughters.

2. _____ Maria has always been difficult.

3. _____ Maria can go to parties alone with her boyfriend if her parents know the family.

4. _____ Being "a good girl" is not as important to Maria as it is to her parents.

5. _____ Jun grew up in the Philippines.

6. _____ None of Maria's friends can go out with boys either.

7. _____ Maria doesn't want to be different from her friends.

8. _____ Maria's friends are from the Philippines.

9. _____ Maria will be able to date when she is 15.

10. _____ If she lived in the Philippines, Maria would be able to go out alone with her boyfriend.

C VOCABULARY

Circle the letter of the choice with the same meaning as the italicized word(s).

1. We have five *kids.*
   a. parents   b. relatives   c. children

2. The PTA is the *Parent*-Teacher Association.
   a. child   b. father or mother   c. president

3. They seem to *grow up* too quickly.
   a. become adults   b. become   c. continue
                               independent

4. Her *reputation* is very important.
   a. the way she lives   b. what people   c. values
                               think about her

5. Do you want me to *pick you up?*
   a. come to get you   b. drive you   c. put you higher

6. Did you always *obey* your parents?
   a. agree with them   b. respect them   c. do what they said

7. She *behaves* differently now that she's a teenager.
   a. lives   b. communicate   c. acts

8. When did they start to *date?*
   a. go out alone together b. change in age   c. feel strongly about
                                                          each other

9. They are completely *out of touch.*
   a. in contact   b. not popular   c. not aware

10. Our *values* are more traditional than theirs.
    a. lifestyles   b. strong beliefs   c. customs

D REACT

Answer the questions or complete the statements. Then share your answers with a classmate or with the class.

1. When I was a teenager, my parents didn't want me to . . . but I . . . .

2. Jun doesn't want Maria to . . . because . . . .

3. Maria wants to . . . because . . . .

4. In my opinion, when a family moves to another culture, the parents should (*follow, not follow*) the customs of the new culture. They (*should, shouldn't*) allow their children to be like other children in that culture.

5. Parents often worry about their children. In your country, what are the three most common things that parents worry about?

__	physical danger	__	education
__	drugs	__	reputation
__	loss of religion	__	teenage pregnancy
__	alcohol	__	gangs
__	violence outside the home		

OTHER PROBLEMS

_____

_____

6. Compare your answers to the answers given by 400 parents who were surveyed by the *Boston Globe* (June 4, 1995).

Crime and violence	39%
Drugs	17%
Economic opportunity	11%
AIDS	4%
Environmental destruction	4%
School system	3%
Other	19%
Don't know	3%

In general, what is your greatest worry about the world in which your children are growing up?

7. In the United States, teenagers usually go through a stage that is very difficult as they try to establish their independence from their parents. Is this "rebellious" stage common in your country?

8. Some parents and teenagers get along better than others. What do you think makes the difference?

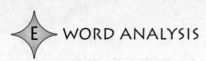 WORD ANALYSIS

PART 1

*Look at the endings for **verbs** and **adjectives**. Are the italicized words in the sentences verbs or adjectives?*

	VERBS	ADJECTIVES
-able	like	lik**able**
	accept	accept**able**

	NOUN	ADJECTIVE
1. Ask anyone. Everyone here is very *knowledgeable*.	_____	_____
2. Her personality *changes* like the wind.	_____	_____
3. That solution is *unthinkable*.	_____	_____
4. What do Americans *value*?	_____	_____
5. He usually has very *changeable* ideas.	_____	_____
6. *Compare* the two cars. They are very similar.	_____	_____
7. This is a very strange place; the weather *changes* almost every hour.	_____	_____
8. Your decision is not *workable*.	_____	_____
9. Those two cars have *comparable* engines.	_____	_____
10. I know what you mean. It's *understandable*.	_____	_____

PART 2

1. Study the meanings of these: Can you think of another example?

trans-	across	**trans**portation **trans**ient	_____
port-	carry	trans**port** ex**port**	_____
ex-, e-	out of, from	**ex**port **e**migrate	_____
im-	into	**im**port **im**migrate	_____
tri-	three	**tri**ple **tri**pod	_____
bi-	two	**bi**noculars **bi**lingual	_____
temp-	time	con**temp**orary **temp**o	_____
mono-	one	**mono**gamy	_____
poly-	many	**poly**gamy	_____

2. Complete the sentences with one of the above words.

   a. They study in two languages at school. It is a _____ school.

   b. When did your parents _____ to the United States?

   c. A big problem in some countries is that the well-educated people
   _____ from those countries instead of staying and
   contributing what they can to the society.

   d. A trading company _____s and _____s things
   from one country to another.

   e. I brought my _____ so I can see everything up close.

   f. John Kennedy and Martin Luther King, Jr. lived at the same time. They
   were _____s.

   g. Professional photographers stand their cameras on _____s.

   h. You are only supposed to have one wife in the United States.
   _____ is the law. In some cultures, you can have more than
   one wife. _____ is permitted.

LOOK BACK

A VOCABULARY

Circle the letter of the choice that best completes each sentence.

1. It increased from 50 to 150. The number __.
   a. declined   b. doubled   c. tripled

2. They never take their children to dinner with them because they __ so badly.
   a. emphasize   b. wait   c. behave

3. A lot of people live in my house, and there is very little __. I can't get away from the other people to be by myself.
   a. privacy   b. noise   c. socializing

4. There is too much crime and __ on television shows today. I think it has a bad influence on children and on adults, too.
   a. divorce   b. privacy   c. violence

5. In the afternoon, a babysitter comes in to __ the children.
   a. raise   b. grow up   c. take care of

6. What is your __ reason for coming here?
   a. primary   b. previous   c. realistic

7. In the __ world, TV is an important means of communication.
   a. contemporary   b. statistical   c. violent

8. This writer always __ descriptions of scenery. I like more action.
   a. prevents   b. emphasizes   c. reshapes

9. I'm sorry, but I'm going to have to __ our meeting. Could you come back on Wednesday?
   a. face   b. establish   c. postpone

10. We always celebrate our holidays in the __ way.
    a. traditional   b. supportive   c. experienced

B MATCHING

Find the word or phrase in column B that has a similar meaning to a word in column A. Write the letter of that word or phrase next to the word in column A.

	A		B
1. ____	reputation	a.	wait to do later
2. ____	neighborhood	b.	repeated action requiring no thought
3. ____	habit	c.	closeness
4. ____	primary	d.	typical
5. ____	town	e.	what people think of someone
6. ____	togetherness	f.	area of places to live
7. ____	sense	g.	set up
8. ____	establish	h.	major
9. ____	postpone	i.	feeling
10. ____	common	j.	very small city

C SYNTHESIS

Work together. *Answer the following questions.*

1. Interview an older person about changes in his/her country's society in the past fifty years. Talk about general changes as well as changes in family life.

2. Choose some aspect of American life (for example, education, bringing up children, crime). Work with a classmate to develop questions about this topic. Interview people, and report back to the class.

D VOCABULARY PREVIEW

What shorter words can you find in these words?

1. Protestant _____

2. percentage _____

3. lifestyles _____

4. useless _____

5. assistance _____

6. retirees _____

7. productive _____

8. retirement _____

9. carefully _____

10. employer _____

11. government _____

12. employees _____

13. What does the "ees" at the end of the words *retirees* and *employees* mean? How is employer different from employee? _____

_____

7 RETIREMENT

A FIRST LOOK

 A BACKGROUND BUILDING

Work together. In groups of three, answer the questions. One student should record (write down) the group's answers.

1. Look at the illustration on the previous page, and answer the following questions.

    a. What are these people doing?

    b. Do you think that they are on vacation?

    c. How old do you think they are?

    d. The word *retire* means to stop working when you are old. What do you think a *retirement city* is?

2. Complete these sentences about your culture.

    a. People usually retire when they are _____.

    b. After retirement, they spend their time _____ing.
                                    (verb)

Report to your class.

B TOPIC

Before you begin to read, look at these topics. There is one topic for each paragraph. Look quickly at the reading to find these topics. Do not read every word at this point. Write the number of the paragraph next to the topic of that paragraph.

1. _____ the financial problems of retirement

2. _____ the value of work in America

3. _____ answers to some problems

4. _____ the positive side of retirement

5. _____ explanation of retirement

RETIREMENT

1   Work is a very important part of life in the United States. When the early Protestant immigrants came to this country, they brought the idea that work was the way to God and heaven. This attitude, the Protestant work ethic, still influences America today. Work is not only important for economic benefits, the salary, but also for social and psychological needs, the feeling of doing something for the good of the society. Americans spend most of their lives working, being productive. For most Americans, their work defines them: They are what they do. What happens, then, when a person can no longer work?

2   Most Americans stop working at age 65 or 70 and retire. Because work is such an important part of life in this culture, retirement can be very difficult. Some retirees feel that they are useless and unproductive. Of course, some people are happy to retire; but leaving one's job, whatever it is, is a difficult change, even for those who look forward to retiring. Many retirees do not know how to use their time, or they feel lost without their jobs.

3   Retirement can also bring financial problems. Many people rely on Social Security checks every month. During their working years, employees contribute a certain percentage of their salaries to the government. Each employer also gives a certain percentage to the government. When people retire, they receive this money as income. These checks do not provide enough money to live on, however, because prices are increasing very rapidly. Senior citizens, those over age 65, have to have savings in the bank or other retirement plans to make ends meet. The rate of inflation is forcing prices higher each year; Social Security checks alone cannot cover these growing expenses. The government offers some assistance, Medicare (health care) and welfare (general assistance), but many senior citizens have to change their lifestyles after retirement. They have to spend carefully to be sure that they can afford to buy food, fuel, and other necessities.

4   Of course, many senior citizens are happy with retirement. They have time to spend with their families or to enjoy their hobbies. Some continue to work part time; others do volunteer work. Some, like those in the Retired Business Executives Association, even help young people to get started in new businesses. Many retired citizens also belong to "Golden Age" groups. These organizations plan trips and social events. There are many opportunities for retirees.

5   American society is only beginning to be concerned about the special   35
physical and emotional needs of its senior citizens. The government is taking   36
steps to ease the problem of limited income. It is building new housing, offering 37
discounts in stores and museums and on buses, and providing other services,   38
such as free classes, food service, and help with housework. Retired citizens are 39
a rapidly growing percentage of the population. This part of the population is   40
very important, and we must respond to its needs. After all, every citizen will be 41
a senior citizen someday.   42

REACT

Underline one interesting idea from the reading. Read it aloud several times to yourself in order to understand its meaning more fully. Then read your sentence to a partner.

D SCANNING/VOCABULARY

PART 1

Write the line number where you find the word(s). Then circle the letter of the choice with the best meaning for the word as it is used in that sentence.

1. work   line number ___
   a. material   b. jobs   c. business

2. influences   line number ___
   a. changes   b. affects   c. compares

3. economic   line number ___
   a. partial   b. financial   c. supportive

4. productive   line number ___
   a. useful   b. unnecessary   c. professional

5. retirement   line number ___
   a. stopping work   b. employment   c. taking a rest

6. employer   line number ___
   a. worker   b. boss   c. business person

7. afford   line number ___
   a. be able to buy   b. contribute   c. prevents

8. volunteer   line number ___
   a. unpaid   b. salaried   c. intentional

9. contribute   line number ___
   a. include   b. take   c. give

10. provide   line number ___
    a. give   b. prepare   c. offer

PART 2

Find a word in the reading that has a meaning similar to the following. The line number is given.

1. line 3   belief   _____
2. line 5   pay   _____
3. line 7   useful   _____
4. line 11   unimportant   _____
5. line 15   depend on   _____
6. line 18   part   _____
7. line 19   salary   _____
8. line 27   needed things _____
9. line 28   older   _____
10. line 35 worried   _____
11. line 38 reduced prices _____
12. line 41 answer   _____

Circle the letter of the choice that best completes each sentence.

1. The author believes that work first became important to Americans because of __ pressure.
   a. economic   b. religious   c. family

2. Protestants believed in __.
   a. high salaries   b. America   c. hard work

3. Senior citizens have to have other savings because Social Security checks __.
   a. are not   b. come monthly   c. cover growing expenses
       enough

4. When Americans stop working, it is difficult for them to __.
   a. feel   b. get Social   c. be religious
      productive   Security checks

5. According to the author, __ Americans stop working at age 65 or 70.
   a. some   b. a few   c. most

6. The author mentions __ examples of discounts.
   a. two   b. three   c. four

7. Some retirees feel useless because they __.
   a. do volunteer   b. have limited   c. aren't working
      work   incomes

8. The last sentence of the reading means that each person __.
   a. is important   b. is a citizen   c. will grow old

9. A salary is a __ benefit.
   a. psychological   b. social   c. financial

10. Many people who retire feel unproductive because their work __.
    a. defined   b. was unimportant   c. was difficult
       their lives

LOOK AGAIN

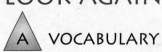

VOCABULARY

Circle the letter of the choice that best completes each sentence.

1. Clothing is an example of a(n) __.
   a. assistance   b. necessity   c. concern

2. It is very late. She is very __ about her son.
   a. productive   b. demanding   c. concerned

3. My __ pays me a good salary.
   a. volunteer   b. employer   c. employee

4. Every year I __ a percentage of my income to my church.
   a. limit   b. receive   c. contribute

5. Every year he __ to work at the school; he never gets paid.
   a. gets by   b. volunteers   c. provides

6. The older children in a family always __ the younger ones.
   a. establish   b. influence   c. define

7. I don't have enough money to buy a new car. I cannot __ one.
   a. demand   b. provide   c. afford

8. Your salary is very low. Do you have any other __?
   a. income   b. interest   c. percentage

9. His physical condition is unbelievable: He's 70 and he __ jogs.
   a. no longer   b. then   c. still

10. He is a __ volunteer here at the hospital; he is a big problem and no help.
    a. productive   b. useful   c. useless

B VOCABULARY/COMPREHENSION

Complete the reading summary with the words from this list. Try to complete it first without looking back at the reading.

retirement	relax	free	hobby	important
work	productive	useless	sixty-five	retire

Generally speaking, Americans (1) _____ until they are (2) _____. Then they (3) _____. (4) _____ can be very difficult for people because their work was so (5) _____ to them. Often people work so much that they do not take the time to (6) _____ or to have a(n) (7) _____. Then when they retire, they don't know what to do with all the (8) _____ time on their hands. They also can feel (9) _____ because they are not being (10) _____. Retirement isn't easy.

C THINK ABOUT IT

Discuss the answers to these questions with a classmate.

1. One problem for senior citizens is financial. List some sources of income that retirees in the U.S. have.

2. Does your country have a Social Security system similar to the one in the United States? How does the system work? Do senior citizens have enough money to live on?

3. Another problem that retirees face is what to do with all their free time. What are some of the activities mentioned in the reading?

4. What do you think are the most serious problems of old age? Write #1 next to the most serious problem for the elderly.

In your home country:

___ financial   ___ physical   ___ psychological   ___ housing

In the United States:

___ financial   ___ physical   ___ psychological   ___ housing

D GRAPH

Age Distribution by Country				
	1994		*2000 (Projected)*	
Selected Countries	*Percentage of the Population under 15 years old*	*Percentage of the Population 65 years old and over*	*Percentage of the Population under 15 years old*	*Percentage of the Population 65 years old and over*
Brazil	31.8	4.5	18.5	5.2
China (PRC)	26.7	6.0	25.1	6.8
Colombia	32.7	4.3	29.9	5.0
Ecuador	36.5	4.2	32.9	4.5
Ethiopia	45.7	3.0	45.8	2.8
Ghana	45.3	3.0	46.1	3.0
India	35.1	3.9	33.3	4.4
Indonesia	33.1	3.4	30.2	4.3
Italy	16.4	15.9	15.5	17.5
Japan	16.6	13.7	15.7	16.5
Mexico	37.7	4.2	34.7	4.8
Poland	23.4	10.9	20.4	12.3
Sweden	16.0	18.0	17.2*	19.5*
Russia	22.3	11.6	20.1	12.6
United Kingdom	19.6	15.8	18.4	15.9
United States	22.0	12.7	21.4	12.7
Vietnam	36.9	4.9	33.9	5.2

Source: U.S. Statistical Abstracts, 1995
*estimated

FIGURE 8

Work in groups of three to answer the questions about differences in aging in various countries throughout the world.

1. In 1994, which of these countries had the largest percentage of people of retirement age?

   _____

2. In 1994, which of these countries had the largest percentage of young people?

   _____

3. Find two countries that will have similar population distribution in the year 2000.

   a. _____   b. _____

4. Find two countries that will have very different population distribution in the year 2000. Explain why.

   a. _____   b. _____

What will these population distributions mean in terms of the elderly and the work force in these countries? List your ideas, and then report the group list to the whole class.

CONTACT A POINT OF VIEW

 BACKGROUND BUILDING

Read these two opinions about retirement. Which is more positive? Which do you think your parents will have when they retire? How about you?

1. "I've never been happier. I finally have time to do all the things that I had always wanted to do."

2. "I have too much time, and I don't always know what to do with myself. I almost never see my friends from work."

B TIMED READING

Read the following point of view, and answer the questions in four minutes.

I retired about a year ago. The company had a big party for me and gave me a gold watch for more than thirty years of service. At the party, everyone said to me, "Retirement is a time to do all the things you didn't have time to do. It's a new beginning." I can't say that I dislike retirement, but after working for thirty-five years, day after day, it's hard to adjust to all this free time.

Just after I retired, Peg and I went to visit John, Jr. in Chicago and Ann in New York. We really had a good time. We enjoy being together. In fact, John, Jr. invited us to come and live with him. He knows that living on Social Security checks and a small retirement plan is not easy. But we decided not to move in with him. We have our lives, and he and his wife have theirs. We are going to stay here in town. We may move to an apartment, because the house is too big for only the two of us, and it's hard to keep clean. Peg is having some trouble with her back; she's seeing the doctor tomorrow.

Money isn't a serious problem for us because we do have some savings, but we have to make careful decisions about what we can afford. We're not used to living on a fixed income, but we make ends meet. I still belong to the club, and I play cards there once a week, and we spend time with other retired couples in the area. My only regret is that I didn't spend enough time thinking about retirement before it happened.

Read the following statements carefully to determine whether each is true (T), false (F), or impossible to know (ITK).

1. _____ This man retired about six months ago.

2. _____ The people at the party were negative about retiring.

3. _____ This man's son is married.

4. _____ This man worked for forty years in the company.

5. _____ He and his wife are moving in with John, Jr.

6. _____ This man dislikes retirement.

7. _____ He and his wife live only on their savings and a retirement plan.

8. _____ This man has other children at home.

9. _____ This man has some physical problems.

10. _____ This man and his wife are going to move from the town.

C VOCABULARY

Fill in the blanks with vocabulary from the reading. Make necessary changes in the form of the words.

1. serious/regret/plans

   I have some _____ _____ about my _____
   to live away from my family.

2. in fact/begin/back/trouble

   Little by little he is _____ to feel better. _____, he has

   no _____ at all with his _____ now.

3. dislike/decisions/money

   I _____ making _____ about _____.

4. limited/afford/make ends meet

   I can't _____ to live on a _____ income because I

   can't _____.

D REACT

Work on your own. *Show your opinion of the following statements by writing* **1** *next to your first preference,* **2** *next to your second choice, and so on through* **6**.

When my parents grow old and retire, I hope that they live

_____ with me.

_____ with my brother.

_____ with my sister.

_____ some time with me, and some time with my brother and/or sister.

_____ near me, so I can visit them.

_____ independently of the family.

It's often a real problem when one parent dies and the other is alone. If my father died, I'm sure that my mother would

_____ continue living where she is living.

_____ move in with me.

_____ live with my brother.

_____ live with my sister.

_____ move to a smaller residence.

_____ move to a nursing home (a home for the elderly).

Work together. *In groups of three or four, share your ideas. Did members of your group agree? In the same group, brainstorm (think up) a list of all the activities you would do if you could retire today. Compare your list with those of the other groups.*

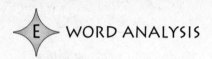

WORD ANALYSIS

PART 1

Choose the appropriate word form for each sentence.

1. special
   specialty

   1. What is the _____ of this restaurant?

2. pain
   painful
   painless

   2. What a _____ in the neck!

3. simple
   simplicity

   3. She is a _____ child.

4. knowledge
   knowledgeable

   4. His _____ of physics surprised me.

5. beneficial
   benefit

   5. It is _____ to visit another country.

6. cultural
   culture

   6. Differences in _____ often cause serious trouble.

7. familiarity
   familiar

   7. I was unaccustomed to the _____ in that society.

8. fear
   fearless
   fearful

   8. He is without _____.

9. impressionable
   impression

   9. She is very young and _____.

10. senseless
    sense

    10. What is the real _____ of this word?

PART 2

1. Study the meanings of these: Can you think of another example?

-er	the subject of the stem	trai**ner**	_____
-ee	the object of the stem	trai**nee**	_____

(Note: *-er* endings are more common than *-ee* endings)

popul-	people	**popul**ation	_____
cent-	hundred	per**cent**age	_____
psych-	the mind	**psych**ological	_____

2. Complete the sentences with one of the above words.

   a. What is the _____ of your city?

   b. Sometimes retirement is a big _____ adjustment. It takes time to get used to it.

   c. In the circus, an animal _____ works very closely with an animal to teach it tricks.

   d. What _____ of the people voted against gun control?

   e. My sister is a _____ in computer programming. She's learning a lot in her classes.

3. Write the meaning of the **boldfaced** word on the line.

   a. The city celebrated its **bicentennial** with a parade and other special activities.

   _____

   b. The man tried to kill his family. He was **psychotic**.

   _____

   c. The **manager** showed the **trainees** around the store.

   _____

   d. The law was extremely **unpopular**.

   _____

LOOK BACK

 A VOCABULARY

Circle the letter of the choice that best completes each sentence.

1. Poverty in a wealthy society is a(n) __ problem.
   a. mobile   b. ethical   c. spacious

2. She is in her last year of high school. She is a __.
   a. junior   b. senior   c. beginner

3. A car is a(n) __ in the suburbs.
   a. aspect   b. establishment   c. necessity

4. Don't worry. Everything will be fine. Heaven will __.
   a. produce   b. provide   c. make ends meet

5. This coat is __. You can buy it for 15 percent off.
   a. salaried   b. increasing   c. discounted

6. The price of food has increased 10 percent in the last month. What __!
   a. development   b. inflation   c. influence

7. I can __ with twenty dollars a day.
   a. afford   b. make ends meet   c. look for

8. This hat is __ in the rain. It's too small and doesn't cover my head.
   a. fixed   b. useless   c. casual

9. Our culture __ our thoughts and actions.
   a. influences   b. gets started   c. contains

10. He's a very good student. __, he's the best in the class.
    a. For example   b. In fact   c. Therefore

MATCHING

Find the word in column B that has a similar meaning to a word in column A.
Write the letter of that word next to the word in column A

	A		B
1. _____	afford	a.	useful
2. _____	provide	b.	affect
3. _____	necessities	c.	value
4. _____	influence	d.	part
5. _____	ethic	e.	needed things
6. _____	financial	f.	be able to buy
7. _____	growing	g.	economic
8. _____	percentage	h.	respond
9. _____	answer	i.	increasing
10. _____	productive	j.	give

SYNTHESIS

Plan a visit to a retirement community. Work with your teacher to arrange your visit. Some possibilities: prepare some entertainment for the people there; become a "conversation partner" with someone there; prepare some snacks for some of the people there, and have some informal discussion with them; ask to interview them about questions you have prepared.

Work together.

1. Think about senior citizens you know or have met in the United States. Are these seniors lonely or unhappy? What do they do in their free time?

2. Think about senior citizens from your country. Are they lonely or unhappy? How do they spend their time?

3. There is a well-known expression in English: "You're only as old as you feel." What do you think this means? Do you agree?

D VOCABULARY PREVIEW

What smaller words can you find in the following words?

1. equalize   _____
2. differences   _____
3. successful   _____
4. equality   _____
5. restrooms   _____
6. protection   _____
7. wealthy   _____
8. upper   _____
9. royalty   _____
10. background   _____
11. powerful   _____
12. minority   _____

E SKIMMING

Look quickly at the next page. Answer these questions.

1. What book is this from?
2. What information is listed?

F SCANNING

Answer these questions as quickly as possible.

1. Find an organization that helps seniors with health problems.
2. Find three organizations that help seniors get good food to eat.
3. Find an organization that helps seniors who cannot drive.
4. Find an organization that helps Indochinese and Chinese senior citizens.
5. Where can seniors go if they want people to socialize with?
6. What is your reaction to the information on the next page?
7. Make a list of services for seniors in your own community.

Senior Citizens Service Organizations (Con't)

ELM BAPTIST CHURCH ————
Sun Sch 8:30 AM-Wor 11 AM & 6 PM
Senior Adults-Wed 10:30 AM-7 PM
Bible Study-Childrens Clubs-Youth
Spanish Speaking Services Available
Rev John Miller-Sr. Pastor
Richard Lee-Assistant Pastor

N 46th & Sunnyside 555-4354

GOLDEN CARE PLUS
Associated With City Hospital
1550 N 115th 555-7587
Green Senior Center 525 N 85th 555-7841
Hampton House for Senior Citizens
5225 15th NE 555-0473
Hanley Nutrition Site 1210 SW 136th . . . 555-5768
Hanley Senior Center 1210 SW 136th . . 555-3686

HOME REPAIRS FOR THE ELDERLY
500 30th St 555-7802

HOMESHARING FOR SENIORS
1601 2nd Ave Suite 800 555-5725
Independent Living 1715 E Cherry 555-3637
Indochina/Chinese Elderly Association
409 Maynard St 555-9577
June Valley Senior Center
105 2nd Ave NE 555-2381

LA EASEL RESTAURANT
2524 16th 555-3837
Lifetime Learning Center 202 John 555-5523
Lifetime Services Inc
800 5th Ave Suite 800 555-8220

MEALS-ON-WHEELS
1601 2nd Ave Suite 800 555-5767
North Senior Center
9929 NE 180th 8th 555-2441
Northwest Senior Center 4429 32 NW . . 555-7811
Norton Day Care For Adults
9250 14th NW 555-8285
Nutrition Projects for Senior Citizens
1601 2d Suite 800 555-5768
Pederson John Social Services
3015 37th SW 555-3020
Red Cross Aid to Aging
1900 25th Av S 555-2345
Senior Center of Weston
4217 SW Oregon 555-4044

SENIOR MEAL PROGRAM
1601 2nd Ave Suite 800 555-5768

SENIOR INFORMATION AND ASSISTANCE
1601 2nd Ave Suite 800 555-3110

SENIOR REFERRAL SERVICE 555-5767
Senior Rights Assistance
1601 2nd Ave Suite 800 555-5720

SENIOR RIGHTS ASSISTANCE
1601 2nd Ave Suite 800 555-5720
Senior Services
211 Burnett N 555-2533

SENIOR SERVICES OF SEATTLE/KING COUNTY
1601 2nd Ave Suite 800 555-5757
Black Diamond
6th &Lawson 555-2418
Bothell
9929 NE 180th 555-2441
Central Area
400-30th Ave S 555-7816
First Hill
800 Jefferson St 555-5748
Greenwood
525 N 85th St 555-7841
Maple Valley
22010 SE248th 555-3222
Northwest
5429-32nd Ave NW 555-7811
Shoreline
835 NE 155th 555-1536
Sno-Valley
Stossel &Commercial Sts 555-4152
Southeast Seattle
7315-39th Ave S 555-0317
Tallmadge Hamilton House
5225-15th Ave NE 555-0473
Vashon-Maury
SW 176th St 555-5173
Wallingford
4649 Sunnyside Ave N 555-7825
West Seattle
4217 SW Oregon St 555-4044
Share the Ride Club P O Box 80325 . . . 555-7881
Shoreline Senior Adult Multi Service Center
835 NE 155th 555-1536
Southeast Seattle Senior Center
4655 S Holly St 555-0317

SPECIALIZED TRANSPORTATION
1601 2nd Ave Suite 800 555-5740
Wallingford Senior Center
4649 Sunnyside N 555-7825
White Center Nutrition Program
9002 16th SW 555-8762

FIGURE 9

8 EQUALITY FOR ALL?

A FIRST LOOK

 A BACKGROUND BUILDING

Look at the illustration on the preceding page, and answer the following questions.

1. What is happening in the illustration?

2. Why have these people come to the White House?

3. How do the protesters feel?

4. What does *equality for all* mean?

5. The following is a quote from the Civil Rights Act of 1964:

   "No person in the United States shall, on the ground of race, color or national origin, be excluded from participation in . . . any program receiving federal financial assistance."

   Explain what this quote means in your own words.

B TOPIC

Before you begin to read, look at these topics. There is one topic for each paragraph. Look quickly at the reading to find these topics. Do not read every word at this point. Write the number of the paragraph next to the topic of that paragraph.

1. _____ American society

2. _____ more about discrimination

3. _____ equal opportunity laws

4. _____ questions about possibilities for minorities

5. _____ definitions of *prejudice* and *discrimination*

6. _____ examples of self-made men

EQUALITY FOR ALL?

1   Can a poor country boy from the hills of Kentucky become President of   1
the United States? Can a poor African American from the center city become   2
wealthy and famous all over the world? Can a woman become President of the   3
United States? The answer to all of these questions is "yes, ideally it is possible."   4
The key word here is *ideally*. Ideally, everyone in the United States, whether rich   5
or poor, has an equal opportunity to succeed.   6

2   This concept of equal opportunity to succeed is a basic idea in capitalism,   7
the economic system of the United States. Social classes or levels are not   8
permanently established. The terms *upper class* or *upper-middle class* are mainly   9
financial terms, although an upper-class person has been wealthy for a long time.   10
There are no kings, queens, or other royalty in the United States, and a person's   11
background is not as important as that person's position. Perhaps because the   12
United States is a country of immigrants, people who often had very little when   13
they arrived in the country, Americans value the ability to go "from rags to   14
riches."   15

3   The first two examples in the first paragraph are descriptions of self-made   16
men, who started life with almost nothing and became successful. These men   17
are President Abraham Lincoln and the boxer Mohammed Ali. These two men   18
did not have the advantages of wealth, good educational opportunities, or   19
contact with powerful people. However, they were ambitious and wanted to   20
succeed.   21

4   Of course, it is unrealistic to say that everyone who wants to succeed will   22
be able to succeed. But there are laws that give every person in the United   23
States the chance or opportunity to succeed. These laws guarantee equal   24
opportunities for education and employment to all people. These laws are   25
especially important to members of minorities (i.e., any group of people not   26
white, Protestant, and male in the United States) such as Hispanics, women,   27
African Americans, people with physical disabilities, and many other ethnic,   28
religious, and racial groups. Minority groups may find that they do not have equal   29
education, housing, or employment. They may have difficulty finding jobs or   30
getting adequate pay because of prejudice.   31

5   *Prejudice* is a negative feeling against a person because of his or her race,   32
religion, or background. For example, if a factory owner does not like Mexican   33
Americans in general, this person is prejudiced. A prejudiced person actually   34

5   prejudges a whole group of people and feels negatively about all the people in   35
that group. If a factory owner feels prejudiced, this is not a problem. The   36
problem arises when the factory owner refuses to hire someone because of   37
that prejudice. If an employer gives a job to a man instead of a woman just   38
because he is a man when both are equally qualified, this is called *discrimination*.   39
Discrimination in housing, education, and employment is illegal in this country.   40

6   The word *discrimination* really means the observation of differences.   41
Obviously, there are differences in people. However, equal opportunity laws try   42
to prevent differences from becoming problems when people want to succeed.   43
In education, employment, and many other areas, discrimination is a bad word.   44

REACT

Underline one sentence that you found interesting in the reading. Read it to a partner.

D SCANNING/VOCABULARY

PART 1

Scan the reading for these words. Write the number of the line where you find them. Then compare the meaning in the sentence to the meaning of the word(s) on the right. Are the words similar or different? Write **similar** or **different** on the line.

	LINE NUMBER		SIMILAR OR DIFFERENT?
1. center city	___	suburbs	D
2. key	___	important	
3. ideally	___	really	
4. equal	___	same	
5. capitalism	___	economic system	
6. background	___	experience	
7. rags	___	riches	
8. guarantee	___	promise	
9. disabilities	___	abilities	
10. prejudice	___	feeling	
11. prevent	___	stop	

PART 2

Find a word in the reading that has a meaning similar to the following. The line number is given.

1. line 6   chance   _____
2. line 6   do well   _____
3. line 8   classes   _____
4. line 9   fixed   _____
5. line 19   benefit   _____
6. line 20   determined   _____
7. line 31   enough   _____
8. line 37   give a job   _____
9. line 39   able   _____
10. line 40   against the law   _____

READING COMPREHENSION

Circle the letter of the choice that best completes each sentence.

1. According to the author, a woman __ become President of the United States.

   a. can never   b. can ideally   c. probably will not

2. Abraham Lincoln and Mohammed Ali were born __.

   a. rich   b. black   c. poor

3. Lincoln and Ali succeeded __ wealth, good educational opportunities, and powerful friends.

   a. because of   b. in order to get   c. without

4. Generally speaking, social classes in the United States are __.

   a. permanently   b. royalty   c. financial divisions
      established

5. It is __ to refuse to give someone a job because of race, religion, or sex.

   a. intelligent   b. illegal   c. guaranteed

6. Americans value the concept of equal opportunity because __.

   a. many Americans   b. Americans like   c. many poor
      are wealthy   money   immigrants became
                                                             rich

7. There __ laws that guarantee equal opportunity.

   a. are no   b. should be   c. are

8. __ is illegal.

   a. Discrimination   b. A minority   c. Prejudice

9. Discrimination is a problem because it does not give people __.

   a. the same chance   b. an easy life   c. prejudice
      to succeed

10. The author thinks that __.

    a. there is equality   b. prejudice   c. discrimination
       in the United States   is illegal   is a serious problem

F READING

Read the following paragraphs, and answer the questions below.

Over 10 percent of the American population has some type of physical or mental disability, and, as our population grows older, this number will increase. Examples of disabilities are serious difficulty walking, seeing, hearing, speaking, and even thinking. Disabilities also include diseases such as cancer, diabetes, and diseases of the muscles, the nervous system, and the heart. Historically, Americans with disabilities have been discriminated against. They have often been isolated and not permitted to participate in the normal course of life.

In 1990, the Americans with Disabilities Act (ADA) was passed. The purpose of this law was to stop discrimination against Americans who are disabled. Public buildings have been changed to assist disabled people. For example, buildings must have a ramp and elevators for people in wheelchairs, and businesses that do not allow animals must permit dogs that lead the blind. The ADA gives people who have severe physical or mental difficulty a chance to participate more fully in American society.

1. Do you study or work with someone who has an obvious physical disability? What activities do you think are particularly difficult for that person?

2. Do you see many disabled people during your usual day? Do you see more disabled people here than you did in your own country?

3. In a small group, walk around some buildings in the area. Examine them in terms of people who might be blind or have heart trouble. What do you see as problems? What do you see that would be helpful?

4. Think about your daily routine starting from when you get up in the morning. If someone who was in a wheelchair was following your schedule, what kind of problems would he or she face?

LOOK AGAIN

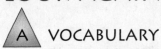

A VOCABULARY

Circle the letter of the choice that best completes each sentence.

1. Laws can __ discrimination but not prejudice.
   a. succeed   b. prevent   c. guarantee

2. A famous person is a person __ knows.
   a. everybody   b. somebody   c. nobody

3. A king and queen are members of __.
   a. immigrants   b. royalty   c. employment

4. __ is not a member of a minority in the United States.
   a. A black Puerto Rican   b. A white male   c. A female

5. The food was adequate. Everyone had __ to eat.
   a. a lot   b. very little   c. the right amount

6. A person who is prejudiced against Hispanics has a(n) __ feeling about them.
   a. negative   b. beneficial   c. advantageous

7. I want a job. Will you __ me in your company?
   a. provide   b. succeed   c. hire

8. She refused. Her answer was __.
   a. positive   b. negative   c. prejudice

9. I bought the house because I plan to live here __.
   a. permanently   b. negatively   c. unrealistically

10. Discrimination in housing means that a landlord does not rent because __.
    a. there is no   b. the people   c. of prejudice
       apartment available   are unpleasant

B READING COMPREHENSION

Complete the following.

1. In paragraph 1, on page 138, the author gives three examples of opportunities to succeed. What are they?

   a. _____

   b. _____

   c. _____

2. In paragraph 2, the author explains the concept of equal opportunity in the United States with two ideas. What are they?

3. What are the names of the two men given as examples in paragraph 3?

4. In what areas do minorities find prejudice?

5. Give one example of prejudice and one of discrimination. Remember that discrimination is an action; prejudice is a feeling.

C THINK ABOUT IT

Answer the following questions.

1. When Irish immigrants first came to Boston, they sometimes read job notices that said "No Irish need apply." Many subsequent groups experienced discrimination. Is there discrimination in your country against immigrants?

2. Why do you think that people discriminate? Why are they prejudiced?

3. Have you ever experienced prejudice or discrimination yourself?

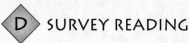

D SURVEY READING

There are laws in the United States to protect people from discrimination and to help them to succeed. In the 1950s, success was a house in the suburbs. Look at Figure 10 below, and answer the questions that follow.

Very Important Elements of Success in America

The numbers on the graph are percentage of respondents who say this is a "very important" element of their idea of success.

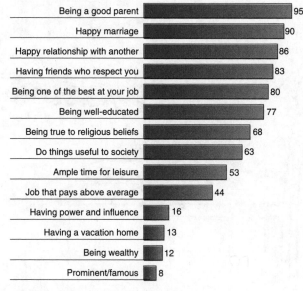

Element	Percentage
Being a good parent	95
Happy marriage	90
Happy relationship with another	86
Having friends who respect you	83
Being one of the best at your job	80
Being well-educated	77
Being true to religious beliefs	68
Do things useful to society	63
Ample time for leisure	53
Job that pays above average	44
Having power and influence	16
Having a vacation home	13
Being wealthy	12
Prominent/famous	8

Source: "The Wall Street Journal/American Dream" survey
conducted by The Roper Organization, February 1987

FIGURE 10

1. What is the most important element of success for Americans according to this survey?
2. According to the survey, do Americans want to be rich and famous?
3. Does the survey show that friendship is important to Americans?
4. Which is more important to Americans according to this survey: good jobs, family, friends, or education? Put these in order of importance (1–4) according to Figure 10.

    _____ good jobs   _____ friends
    _____ family   _____ education

5. What does success mean to you? Number the following in order of importance for you. Write **1** next to the most important, and **2** next to the second most important, and so forth.

    For me, success means having . . .

    _____ a lot of money.   _____ children.
    _____ a good job.   _____ a home.
    _____ friends.   _____ a car.
    _____ a husband or wife.

CONTACT A POINT OF VIEW

A BACKGROUND BUILDING

1. Look at the picture. Who are the two people?

2. What does the man mean by pointing his finger toward the door?

3. In the United States, when can you ask an employee to leave his or her job? How about in your country?

B TIMED READING

Read the following point of view and answer the questions in four minutes.

Silvia Garcia applied for a job at a small company. One question on the application form was "Who else lives at your home address?" Ms. Garcia did not answer this question. She left the space blank.

The owner of the company, Jeff Erler, was a very religious man. He had started the company himself and felt that his employees were like his extended family. Mr. Erler interviewed Ms. Garcia personally. He noticed that she had marked "single" on her application, and he was surprised that she was not married at her age. When he mentioned this to her, she just laughed and did not comment. He decided that she was a very nice woman. He also needed to hire members of minorities, so he was pleased to hire her.

Ms. Garcia did very well in the company. In a few months, she got a raise and was happy with the additional money. However, seven months after Mr. Erler hired her, he overheard a conversation in the cafeteria. Two other workers were talking about her and "the guy she's living with."

Mr. Erler called Ms. Garcia into his office that afternoon. He questioned her about her living situation, and she admitted that she was living with her boyfriend. Mr. Erler told her that he was very sorry, but he did not want immoral people to work in his company. At first, she could not believe that Mr. Erler was serious. She told him that he had no right to call her immoral because she was living with her boyfriend. She said that as long as she was a good worker, her personal life was her own business and that he could not make judgments about it. Mr. Erler fired Ms. Garcia.

1. _____ Ms. Garcia was a member of a minority group.
2. _____ When Ms. Garcia applied for the job, she lived with her boyfriend.
3. _____ Ms. Garcia was not a good worker.
4. _____ Mr. Erler was a religious man.
5. _____ All of Mr. Erler's employees were religious.
6. _____ Ms. Garcia's boyfriend worked in the same company.
7. _____ No one at the company except Mr. Erler knew that Ms. Garcia was living with someone.
8. _____ Ms. Garcia told Mr. Erler that she was not living with her boyfriend.
9. _____ Ms. Garcia was thirty years old.
10. _____ Ms. Garcia lost her job at Mr. Erler's company.

C VOCABULARY

Circle the letter of the choice with the same meaning as the italicized word(s).

1. Who *else* lives at this address?
   a. related   b. in addition   c. only

2. The page was *blank*.
   a. empty   b. written   c. full

3. Leave a *space* between the lines of our compositions.
   a. meaning   b. certain area   c. sentence

4. I *applied* for a loan at the bank.
   a. questioned   b. gave money   c. tried to get

5. A politician often says, *"No comment."*
   a. I have nothing to say.   b. I don't know.   c. Don't talk to me.

6. Our office *hired* someone just yesterday.
   a. fired   b. gave more   c. gave a job to
                        money to

7. I spoke with the director *personally*.
   a. myself   b. quickly   c. immediately

8. Her *personal* life is very interesting.
   a. social   b. private   c. love

9. If he steals money from poor people, he is *immoral*.
   a. rich   b. arrested   c. without values

10. I need a *raise*. I cannot support myself with this salary.
    a. job   b. higher pay   c. vacation with
                        for the same job   more money

D REACT

Reread the information about Silvia Garcia and Jeff Erler. Then answer the following questions, and share your ideas with the class.

1. What do you think Ms. Garcia does next?

    _____ collects unemployment insurance?

    _____ looks for another job?

    _____ goes to see a lawyer?

    _____ _____?

2. Do you think that Mr. Erler was fair to Ms. Garcia?

3. Do you think that Mr. Erler did anything illegal when he fired her?

4. Did Mr. Erler discriminate against her because of:

    her race?
    her sex?
    her religion?
    her personal background?
    her moral values?

5. Do you think this is discrimination? Is it an unfair employment procedure?

If you decide that this case is an example of discrimination or unfair employment procedures, take it to court. Act out the parts of these people:

Silvia Garcia

Steve Kennedy, Silvia's boyfriend

Jeff Erler

Alice Lee, Jeff's secretary

The lawyers who help Silvia Garcia

The lawyers who help Jeff Erler

A judge, who also organizes the trial

A jury of people who decide the final judgment

Step 1: Meet in groups to decide what roles and positions you will take.

Step 2: Meet in court, and present the evidence.

Step 3: Wait for the jury's decision.

F WORD ANALYSIS

PART 1

*Look at the endings below for nouns and verbs. Are the italicized words in the sentences **nouns** or **verbs**?*

Nouns	Verbs
produc**tion**	produce
adjust**ment**	adjust
real**ity**	real**ize**

	Nouns	Verbs
1. I'll help you *familiarize* yourself with the city.	___	___
2. *Discrimination* in hiring is illegal.	___	___
3. How did you *solve* that problem?	___	___
4. Could you *repeat* that please?	___	___
5. I made an *adjustment* in the plan.	___	___
6. I don't have a *solution* to that problem.	___	___
7. His *identity* is still a question.	___	___
8. What is your *community* like?	___	___
9. We can't *produce* that many machines.	___	___
10. Can you *identify* the problem?	___	___

PART 2

1. Study the meanings of these: Can you think of another example?

judi-	judge	pre**judi**ce	_____
pre-	before	**pre**register	_____
post-	after	**post**pone	_____
equ-	equal	ade**qu**ate	_____
leg-	law	**leg**islature	_____

2. Complete the sentences with one of the above words.

   a. They never finished the project because the money the government gave for the project wasn't _____.

   b. The _____ made a decision when they met last month.

   c. If you don't _____ for next semester, you will have to wait in long lines when classes start.

   d. The landlord wouldn't let her rent the apartment when he found out she was a student. She felt that this was _____.

   e. I hate to do my homework, so I usually _____ it for as long as possible.

3. Write the meaning of the **boldfaced** word on the line.

   a. There are some **inequities** in the new tax law, but I'm sure the government will work them out eventually. _____

   b. The **judge** hasn't made a decision yet in the case.

   _____

   c. I got a ticket for parking in an **illegal** space. _____

   d. I can't **prevent** you from going there, but I think you're making a mistake. _____

   e. I'd like to do **postgraduate** work in biochemistry.

   _____

LOOK BACK

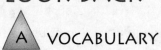

VOCABULARY

Circle the letter of the choice that best completes each sentence.

1. The __ man did not like his daughter's boyfriend because he was Chinese.
   a. prejudiced   b. advantageous   c. adequate

2. I don't know if this color is green or gray. I don't have very good color __.
   a. prejudice   b. discrimination   c. equality

3. There were two men and twelve women in the class. The men were in the __.
   a. minority   b. percentage   c. opportunity

4. I found a job easily because my father __ me to work for him.
   a. hired   b. gave   c. refused

5. I decided to quit before the owner __ me.
   a. raised   b. fired   c. felt

6. With a degree in business, she was highly __ to work in the company.
   a. qualified   b. adequate   c. prejudiced

7. There is a six-month __ on this radio. If it breaks in that time, you can get another one for free.
   a. age   b. guarantee   c. qualification

8. I __ a raise. I don't know if I will get one or not.
   a. prevented   b. fired   c. applied for

9. I can't __ him. He doesn't answer his phone.
   a. adjust to   b. contact   c. give

10. I am very __. I want to succeed and be at the top of my profession.
    a. ambitious   b. economic   c. self-made

B MATCHING

Find the word in column B that has a similar meaning to a word in column A. Write the letter of that word next to the word in column A

	A	B
1. _____	succeed	a. smaller group
2. _____	illegal	b. not legal
3. _____	opportunity	c. give a job to
4. _____	minority	d. enough
5. _____	refuse	e. chance
6. _____	adequate	f. do well
7. _____	hire	g. say no
8. _____	employee	h. even though
9. _____	although	i. the same
10. _____	equal	j. worker in a company or business

C SYNTHESIS

Work together.

Who Does What?	Percentage of various groups in specific jobs.							
	White Men		Blacks		Hispanics		Women	
	1983	1993	1983	1993	1983	1993	1983	1993
Secretaries	.8	.9	5.8	8.4	4.0	6.2	99.0	98.8
Engineers	86.8	82.6	2.7	3.7	2.2	3.3	5.8	8.3
Doctors	74.2	66.1	3.3	4.1	4.4	5.1	15.8	22.3
Lawyers	82.0	73.0	2.6	3.3	.8	3.0	15.2	24.6
Airline Pilots	97.1	92.3	0	1.9		0	1.4	2.9

Source: U.S. Department of Labor

FIGURE 11

What information in Figure 11 surprises you?

VOCABULARY PREVIEW

Circle all the words you can find below. Most of the words are from Chapter 9.

unjustpotmnesacaientreqppitdiscriminationmfeirnprejudiceseparatelecaqillegalwo
minqualifiedseriousgamitovblacksmubvetumidanpersistbinocitaminminoritydunca
colamprotectionheritagenolitdisadvantageinequalityraminracialslavestinompartici
pation

9 RACIAL ISSUES

A FIRST LOOK

 BACKGROUND BUILDING

Racial issues are very deep and complex. Think about your own experience with people from races different from your own by answering this survey.

About your childhood . . . . *Circle the answer.*

1. When I was a child, I lived in a neighborhood that was racially _____.
   a. mixed   b. all the same

2. My childhood friends were from _____.
   a. my race   b. other races

3. My school was racially _____.
   a. mixed   b. all the same

4. As a child, I _____ saw people who were from a different race.
   a. often   b. sometimes   c. almost never

About now . . . . *Circle the answer.*

1. The neighborhood I live in today is racially _____.
   a. mixed   b. all the same

2. I have friends _____.
   a. from many   b. mainly from my race   c. only from my race
   different races

3. I work/study with people _____.
   a. from many   b. mainly from my race   c. only from my race
   different races

TOPIC

Before you begin to read, look at these topics. There is one topic for each paragraph. Look quickly at the reading to find these topics. Do not read every word at this point. Write the number of the paragraph next to the topic of that paragraph.

1. _____ prejudice in the South

2. _____ prejudice and discrimination are problems in the United States

3. _____ equal education

4. _____ time is the answer

5. _____ discrimination in the North

6. _____ equal employment

7. _____ blacks compared to other groups

C READING

Now read.

RACIAL ISSUES

1   Ironically, in the United States—a country of immigrants—prejudice and   1
discrimination continue to be serious problems. There was often tension   2
between each established group of immigrants and each succeeding group. As   3
each group became more financially successful and more powerful, they   4
excluded newcomers from full participation in the society. Prejudice and   5
discrimination are part of our history; however, this prejudicial treatment of   6
different groups is nowhere more unjust than with African Americans.   7

2   African Americans had distinct disadvantages. For the most part, they   8
came to the "land of opportunity" as slaves, and they were not free to keep   9
their heritage and cultural traditions. Unlike most European immigrants, slaves   10
did not have the protection of a support group; sometimes slave owners   11
separated members of the same family. Even after African Americans became   12
free people, they could not mix easily with the established society because of   13
their skin color. They experienced discrimination in employment, housing,   14
education, and even in public facilities, such as restrooms.   15

3   Until the twentieth century (1900s), the majority of African Americans   16
lived in the southern part of the United States. Then there was a population   17
shift to the large cities in the North. Prejudice against African Americans is   18
often associated with the South. Slavery was more common there, and   19
discrimination was usually more blatant (easier to see): Water fountains,   20
restrooms, and restaurants were often designated "white only."   21

4   In the North, discrimination was usually less obvious, but certainly it   22
created poor African American neighborhoods in many center cities. This   23
happened because of discrimination in housing and the movement of white city   24
residents to the suburbs, often called "white flight."   25

5   In the 1950s and 1960s, African Americans fought to gain fair treatment   26
and legal protection in housing, education, and employment. Because their   27
neighborhoods were segregated, many African Americans felt that educational   28
opportunities were not adequate for their children. Busing children from their   29
home neighborhood to other neighborhoods that had better schools and better   30
teachers was one solution to inequality in education. Naturally, all parents want   31
the best possible education for their children.   32

6   One attempt to equalize employment and educational opportunities for all   33
minorities is "affirmative action." Affirmative action means that those in charge   34

6 of businesses, organizations, and institutions should take affirmative (positive)   35
action to find minorities to fill jobs. Many whites are angry about this regulation,   36
because very qualified people sometimes do not get jobs when they are filled by   37
people from a certain minority. People call this practice "reverse discrimination."   38

7   African Americans and other racial minorities have more opportunities   39
today than they did in the 1950s, but racial tension persists. Time will be the   40
real solution to the problem of race.   41

REACT

Look at line 9 of the reading. The author says that African Americans came to the "land of opportunity" as slaves. Why are the words "land of opportunity" in quotes?

D SCANNING/VOCABULARY

PART 1

Write the line number where you find the word(s). Then circle the letter of the choice with the best meaning for the word as it is used in that sentence.

1. ironically   line number ___

   a. unexpectedly   b. naturally   c. obviously

2. succeeding   line number ___

   a. coming before   b. successful   c. following

3. excluded   line number ___

   a. prevented   b. prejudiced   c. adjusted

4. heritage   line number ___

   a. property   b. cultural past   c. work

5. protection   line number ___

   a. conflict   b. involvement   c. safety

6. majority   line number ___

   a. a large   b. some   c. most
       number

7. associated with   line number ___

   a. compared to   b. connected with   c. qualified for

8. attempt   line number ___

   a. gain   b. guarantee   c. effort

9. qualified   line number ___

   a. capable   b. hired   c. ambitious

10. reverse   line number ___

    a. opposite   b. done again   c. prevented

PART 2

Find a word that is the opposite of the one given. The line number is given.

1. line 3   new   _____

2. line 7   fair   _____

3. line 8   benefits   _____

4. line 9   free people   _____

5. line 12   mixed   _____

6. line 20   hidden   _____

7. line 27   unlawful   _____

8. line 28   mixed by race   _____

9. line 31   fairness   _____

10. line 37   inexperienced   _____

READING COMPREHENSION

Circle the letter of the choice that best completes each sentence.

1. Because of __, African Americans could not easily mix in American society.
   a. skin color   b. language   c. heritage

2. Special restrooms and water fountains for African Americans were more common in __.
   a. the North   b. city centers   c. the South

3. __ is one attempt to equalize education.
   a. Reverse discrimination   b. White flight   c. Busing

4. African Americans were different from other groups because they __.
   a. came with the first settlers   b. adapted easily   c. did not choose to come here

5. There __ discrimination in the North.
   a. was   b. wasn't   c. was no

6. According to the author, there will be a solution to racial problems __.
   a. in the future   b. very soon   c. because of the 1950s

7. Affirmative action is most beneficial for __.
   a. minorities   b. business   c. qualified people

8. In the North, discrimination was __ to see.
   a. easier   b. more difficult   c. less difficult

9. The author thinks that prejudice and discrimination are __ in the United States.
   a. natural   b. the same for all groups   c. part of history

10. The author thinks that prejudice is ironic here because the United States is a country of __.
    a. wealth   b. immigrants   c. established groups

LOOK AGAIN

 A VOCABULARY

Circle the letter of the choice that best completes each sentence.

1. I love to eat; __, I hate to cook.
   a. ironically   b. naturally   c. financially

2. One __ of city living is the high cost.
   a. advantage   b. benefit   c. disadvantage

3. He was __ from the club because of his religious beliefs.
   a. participated   b. excluded   c. designated

4. Whites in the United States are the __.
   a. minority   b. majority   c. newcomers

5. The cruel __ of slaves in the United States is difficult to believe.
   a. treatment   b. protection   c. heritage

6. Although she didn't like him, he __ in calling her.
   a. associated   b. persisted   c. designated

7. Busing is a(n) __ to equalize educational opportunities.
   a. loss   b. attempt   c. participation

8. __ public schools are not legal.
   a. Integrated   b. Associated   c. Segregated

9. He is __ to teach economics.
   a. adequate   b. qualified   c. obvious

10. __ discrimination is clear and easy to see.
    a. Reverse   b. Blatant   c. Unjust

READING COMPREHENSION

1. Compare African Americans to other groups who came to the United States. Give two examples of disadvantages that they had.

2. Give two examples of discrimination against African Americans.

3. Reread the information about equality in education, and try to explain what busing means.

THINK ABOUT IT

Discuss the following questions with your classmates.

Is there discrimination in your country? Is it racial? Social? Or sexual? What kind of discrimination takes place? Employment? Housing? Education?

READING

Study the following graph, and answer the questions below.

Median Income of Families by Race and Ethnic Origin 1992				
All Families	**White**	**African American**	**Asian/ Pacific Islanders**	**Hispanic**
$36,812	$38,909	$21,161	$42,556	$23,901

Source: U.S. Statistical Abstracts, 1994
* Median means that 50% earned below that figure and 50% above.

FIGURE 12

1. What does the chart describe?

2. a. Which group has the highest median income?

   b. Which group has the lowest median income?

3. How do you explain the differences in income across the four groups?

 BACKGROUND BUILDING

Affirmative action policies are difficult to understand. These policies suggest that each organization should reflect the total population. For example, African Americans make up about 15 percent of the population in the United States. If you own a small company with 100 employees, how many should be African American?

TIMED READING

In the early 1970s, Allen Bakke, an engineer from California, decided that he wanted to change his career and become a doctor. He applied to the medical school at the University of California. Bakke was a good student; he had graduated from the University of Minnesota with an A average and had a master's degree from Stanford. He was not accepted by the University of California. He was very upset.

Bakke discovered that the university had an affirmative action policy; he believed that some black students who were accepted to the medical school were not as qualified as he was. In other words, he felt that they were accepted because of their race and not because of their background. It seems that the university was trying to equalize opportunities for minority students who had not had equal educational opportunities. The university hoped that by accepting a certain number of minority students they could change a long history of discrimination. Many people believe that in the long run, education will equalize our society.

Bakke felt that this affirmative action policy was unjust and that he had a right to attend medical school. He felt that he was better qualified and that the action of the medical school was reverse discrimination. He considered the action illegal and decided to bring his problem to the court for a decision.

He brought the issue to two state courts in California. The decision of the judges was that the action of the medical school was perfectly legal and that Bakke had to accept this decision.

He then decided to bring the problem to the United States Supreme Court, where the final decision-making power in the United States lies. What do you think happened?

Read the following statements carefully to determine whether each is true (T), false (F), or impossible to know (ITK).

1. _____ Bakke's background was better than most others.
2. _____ Bakke had a good background.
3. _____ Bakke applied to Stanford Medical School.
4. _____ This case happened last year.
5. _____ Reverse discrimination means not accepting minorities.
6. _____ The Supreme Court makes final decisions about laws in the United States.
7. _____ Bakke had no alternative after the decision of the two lower (state) courts.
8. _____ The policy of the school was to fill all places with minority students.
9. _____ The two state courts said that the action was illegal.
10. _____ Bakke accepted the decision of the state courts.

C VOCABULARY

Fill in the blanks with vocabulary from the reading.

1. applied/accepted/attended

   Allen Bakke _____ the University of Minnesota as an

   undergraduate. He _____ to the University of California but

   was not _____ .

2. discrimination/judge/illegal

   The _____ considered that _____ in any form was

   _____ .

3. applicants/accepted/backgrounds

   _____ who had _____ that were not as good as

   Bakke's were _____ .

4. policy/attempt

   This _____ was an _____ to equalize opportunities.

D REACT

Mr. Bakke's affirmative action case is a difficult one. According to the facts, what would you decide? Work in groups of five, and decide the case as the Supreme Court did. Remember that you must have a majority decision (3 to 2). After reaching your decision, present it to the class. Here is some useful vocabulary.

We feel that . . . .

We agree that . . . .

Mr. Bakke should . . . .   legal/illegal

The university should . . . .   necessary/unnecessary

All applicants should . . . .   unconstitutional

Minority applicants must . . . .

Racial discrimination . . . .

Reverse discrimination . . . .

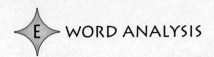 WORD ANALYSIS

PART 1

Choose the appropriate word form for each sentence. Is it a noun or a verb?

1. employ
   employment
1. She is looking for _____.

2. Discriminate
   Discrimination
2. _____ is unfortunately part of the history of this country.

3. treat
   treatment
3. What is the best way to _____ a cold?

4. educate
   education
4. Public schools should _____ everybody.

5. protect
   protection
5. Don't worry. I'll _____ you.

6. equalize
   equality
6. Is the basis of democracy _____?

7. associate
   association
7. She denies any _____ with him.

8. designate
   designation
8. The _____ of "white only" facilities is now over.

9. act
   action
9. They always _____ naturally.

10. solve
    solution
10. Time isn't going to _____ this problem.

PART 2

*In other chapters, you have studied parts of the **boldfaced** words in the following sentences. Write the letter of the correct meaning of the boldfaced word from the list below.*

a. look at before

b. opinion

c. fair

d. story about your own life

e. mental

f. able to be seen

g. come between

h. way out

i. not able to be seen

j. good, positive

1. They asked the government to **intervene** because the two groups couldn't come to any agreement. _____

2. He walked right past me as if I were **invisible**. _____

3. All I want is an **equitable** solution to the problem. _____

4. I'm going to **preview** the movie I'm planning to show in class tomorrow. _____

5. I read that woman's **autobiography**. It was quite interesting. _____

6. Where's the **exit** to this building? _____

7. In my **judgment**, the driver was wrong. _____

8. I think he needs **psychiatric** help. _____

9. His leg was **visible** sticking out from behind the sofa. _____

10. Exercise has **beneficial** effects on your body and mind. _____

LOOK BACK

A VOCABULARY

Circle the letter of the choice that best completes each sentence.

1. The woman did not want the magazines, but the salesperson was __.
   a. exclusive   b. protective   c. persistent

2. This paper from the state court is filled with __.
   a. tension   b. legalities   c. loss

3. She has everything in order: She __ her work very carefully.
   a. segregates   b. organizes   c. associates

4. She makes all the important company decisions, all the __ ones.
   a. reverse   b. major   c. minor

5. It is __ to do that now. Don't wait, or it will be too late.
   a. blatant   b. advantageous   c. succeeding

6. __ speaking, I don't understand the situation at all.
   a. Unjustly   b. Continuously   c. Seriously

7. He __ the word *football* with Americans.
   a. associates   b. participates   c. discriminates

8. Cats are very __ of their kittens.
   a. protective   b. serious   c. affirmative

9. He has improved 100 percent. He has made great __.
   a. attempts   b. gains   c. losses

10. He has very __ taste; only the best for him.
    a. regulatory   b. discriminating   c. common

MATCHING

Find the word or phrase in column B that has a similar meaning to a word in column A. Write the letter of that word or phrase next to the word in column A.

	A		B
1. ____	naturally	a.	unfair
2. ____	disadvantage	b.	positive
3. ____	adequate	c.	tied with
4. ____	legal	d.	different
5. ____	participation	e.	enough
6. ____	segregate	f.	obviously
7. ____	unjust	g.	problem
8. ____	qualified	h.	lawful
9. ____	associated	i.	continue
10. ____	serious	j.	able
11. ____	majority	k.	important
12. ____	distinct	l.	larger percentage
13. ____	persist	m.	involvement
14. ____	affirmative	n.	separate

C SYNTHESIS

Work together. *Read the following three questions and choose the one that interests you most. Join group 1, 2 or 3 to work on the task.*

1. In the 1960s, the now famous case of Rosa Parks occurred. She was a black woman who lived in Montgomery, Alabama. One day she refused to give up her seat on the bus and move to the back. She was arrested. Can that happen today? Find out more about Rosa Parks.

2. In many places in the world, there are all-male private clubs. How do you feel about all-male clubs? Find out if these are possible in the United States.

3. The Ku Klux Klan is an anti-black organization in the United States. Its members are prejudiced against African Americans. Why do you think this group exists? Is this group legal in the United States?

D VOCABULARY PREVIEW

What shorter words can you see in these words from Chapter 10?

1. homemaker   _____
2. uncivilized   _____
3. alongside   _____
4. industrialized   _____
5. postwar   _____
6. inventions   _____
7. generalize   _____
8. nontraditional   _____
9. essentially   _____
10. residential   _____
11. dishwasher   _____
12. undeveloped   _____

10 THE ROLE OF WOMEN IN THE UNITED STATES

A FIRST LOOK

 A BACKGROUND BUILDING

1. Complete these sentences about your country or culture.

    a. Forty years ago, a woman's life in my country (was/was not) different

       from a woman's life now because _____.

    For example, _____.

    b. Some typical jobs for women now are: _____

       _____.

    c. In most families, __ takes care of the children during the day.
       a. the mother   b. a relative   c. someone else

2. Look at the illustration on the previous page. What is the young woman thinking about?

B TOPIC

Write the topic of each paragraph in the reading. Do not write long sentences. Short phrases are fine.

1. _____

2. _____

3. _____

4. _____

5. _____

6. _____

THE ROLE OF WOMEN IN THE UNITED STATES

1 American women experience a great variety of lifestyles. A "typical" American woman may be single. She may also be divorced or married. She may be a homemaker, a doctor, or a factory worker. It is very difficult to generalize about American women. However, one thing that many American women have in common is their attitude about themselves and their role in American life.

2 Historically, American women have always been very independent. The first colonists to come to New England were often young couples who had left behind their extended family (i.e., their parents, sisters, cousins, etc.). The women were alone in a new, undeveloped country with their husbands. This had two important effects. First of all, this as yet uncivilized environment demanded that every person share in developing it and in fighting for their own survival. Women worked alongside their husbands and children to establish themselves in this new land. Second, because they were in a new land without the established influence of older members of society, women felt free to step into nontraditional roles. In addition, there were no rules in the Protestant religion which demanded that women stay in any definite role.

3 This role of women was reinforced in later years as Americans moved west, again leaving family behind and encountering a hostile environment. Even later, in the East, as new immigrants arrived, women often found jobs more easily than men. With jobs such as cleaning, cooking, or sewing, many women became the supporters of the family. The children of these early Americans grew up with many examples of working women around them.

4 Within the established lifestyle of industrialized twentieth-century America, the strong role of women was not as dramatic as in the early days of the country. Some women were active outside the home; others were not. However, when American men went to war in the 1940s, women stepped into the men's jobs as factory and business workers. After the war, some women stayed in these positions, and others left their jobs with a new sense of their own capabilities.

5 When men returned from the war and the postwar "baby boom" began, Americans began to move in great numbers to the suburbs. A new model of a traditional family developed, and women were essentially separated from men. Men generally went back into the city to work, and there was a strong division between work and home. Houses in the suburbs were far apart from each

5 other, and those areas were all residential; there were no stores or businesses. 35
Women had to drive to buy food and to visit family and friends. All these factors 36
contributed to a sense of isolation and to a feeling of separation between the 37
family and the outside world. At the same time technological developments gave 38
American homemakers many time-saving inventions such as dishwashers, 39
vacuum cleaners, and frozen foods. Life became easier for American 40
homemakers but not necessarily more satisfying. With more time on their 41
hands, American women began to want to become more involved. 42

6   Many people think that the women's movement, a political and social effort 43
to give women the same status and rights as men, was a result of this isolation 44
and separation of women in the suburbs. Given the historical model of women 45
who were active outside the home in building America, it is really not surprising 46
that American women are working to reestablish their strong role in American 47
life. 48

REACT

Underline some information that surprised you in the reading. Share this
with a partner.

*Scan the reading for these words. Write the number of the line where you find each word. Then compare its meaning in the sentence to the meaning of the word(s) on the right. Are the words similar or different? Write **similar** or **different** on the line.*

		LINE NUMBER			SIMILAR OR DIFFERENT?
1.	lifestyle		way of life		S
2.	divorced		married		D
3.	attitude		feeling		
4.	couple		two people		
5.	uncivilized		undeveloped		S
6.	share		work together		
7.	definite		general		
8.	reinforced		strengthened		S
9.	hostile		friendly		D
10.	positions		jobs		
11.	capabilities		abilities		S
12.	division		separation		
13.	far apart		close together		D
14.	contribute		add		
15.	satisfying		boring		D

E ▸ READING COMPREHENSION

Circle the letter of the choice that best completes each sentence.

1. The author thinks that there are __ for American women.
   a. few possibilities   b. many choices   c. sometimes jobs

2. American women have felt independent __.
   a. only recently   b. for several   c. since World War II
                                     hundred years

3. Traditions were __ survival in this new land.
   a. as important as   b. less important   c. only for
                                 than

4. American women __ west with their husbands.
   a. did not go   b. left   c. moved

5. In the early twentieth century, __ American women worked.
   a. some   b. all   c. no

6. The move to the suburbs took place in the __.
   a. 1700s   b. 1800s   c. 1900s

7. According to the author, life in the suburbs had a __ effect on women.
   a. positive   b. negative   c. hostile

8. A __ was absolutely necessary in the suburbs.
   a. business   b. car   c. baby boom

9. Technological developments gave women more __.
   a. time   b. satisfaction   c. hands

10. The author feels that the women's movement has __ a strong role for women.
    a. reestablished   b. worked for   c. worked against

LOOK AGAIN

A VOCABULARY

Circle the letter of the choice that best completes each sentence.

1. When there is little variety, people have __.
   a. no time   b. few choices   c. a lot of diversity

2. The student had a negative attitude about her work. She __.
   a. hated it   b. studied hard   c. tried a lot

3. A __ is an example of a timesaver.
   a. watch   b. dishwasher   c. bed

4. They lived a long way from other people. Their home was __.
   a. undeveloped   b. alone   c. isolated

5. The young people felt that they needed no help from anyone. They were very __.
   a. influenced   b. independent   c. uncivilized

6. A residential area has __.
   a. stores   b. houses   c. businesses

7. I __ difficulties in language when I traveled to Russia.
   a. encountered   b. established   c. contributed to

8. The young people tried hard. They showed a lot of __.
   a. effort   b. status   c. influence

9. I __ ten dollars to the organization.
   a. reinforced   b. shared   c. contributed

10. We make the same salaries, but our __ is not the same because you have the title of "director."
    a. status   b. sense   c. model

READING COMPREHENSION

Complete this outline of the reading.

Paragraph 1

This paragraph states that (circle the letter of the answer):

a. All American women are similar.

b. It is hard to make generalizations about American women.

Paragraph 2

Some reasons why women worked hard and stepped into nontraditional roles:

_____

_____

_____

Paragraph 3

Another reason why women had strong roles:

_____

Paragraph 4

In the twentieth century, _____

until _____ when _____.

Paragraph 5

Some reasons why women wanted to get more involved:

_____

_____

_____

Paragraph 6

Conclusion: _____

_____

C THINK ABOUT IT

Discuss the answers to these questions with a classmate.

1. **Fact or opinion?** Read the following statements. Write *fact* or *opinion* next to each one.

   a._____ Fifty-one percent of the American population is female.

   b._____ Men are not good at caring for children.

   c. _____ Women make better doctors than men because they are more sensitive.

2. Go back to the reading.

   a. Find two facts and underline them.

   b. Find one opinion. Underline it.

   c. Find out if your classmates agree about whether they are facts or opinions.

3. Read these paragraphs. Choose only one word or phrase from each box to give your opinion or information about your country or culture. Discuss your ideas with a classmate.

   should—something is a good idea.   *I should get enough sleep.*

   have to—something is necessary.   *I have to take an exam tomorrow.*

   be supposed to—a law, a rule,   *They are supposed to meet me here.*
   agreement

   We aren't supposed to smoke in this room.

   In my opinion, there | should / should not | be | any / some | changes regarding

   women's rights. In my | country / area / culture | women | want to / do not want to / can / cannot | work, | and / but |

   | few / many | do. I think that women | should / should be able to / should not | have a job besides their

   work at home. | They should / should not have to / should not | stay at home to take care of the

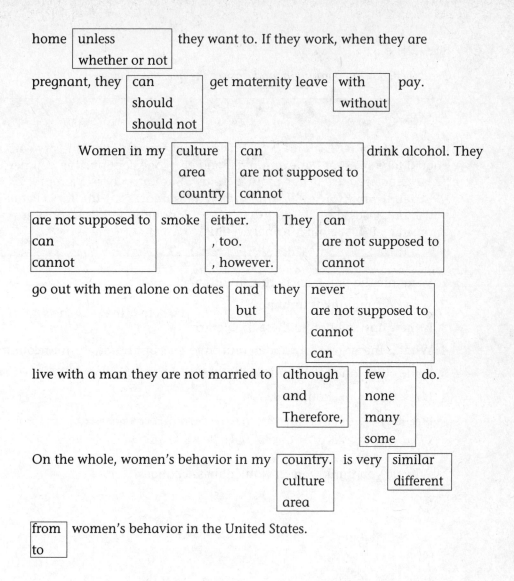

home | unless / whether or not | they want to. If they work, when they are

pregnant, they | can / should / should not | get maternity leave | with / without | pay.

Women in my | culture / area / country | can / are not supposed to / cannot | drink alcohol. They

| are not supposed to / can / cannot | smoke | either. / , too. / , however. | They | can / are not supposed to / cannot |

go out with men alone on dates | and / but | they | never / are not supposed to / cannot / can |

live with a man they are not married to | although / and / Therefore, | few / none / many / some | do.

On the whole, women's behavior in my | country. / culture / area | is very | similar / different |

| from / to | women's behavior in the United States.

READING

Read the following paragraph, and answer the questions below.

Margaret Lee and Peter Erickson got married a couple of years ago. Margaret kept her own name, and everyone continued to call her Margaret Lee except her mother-in-law. She introduces Margaret as Margaret Erickson and sends her letters addressed to "Mrs. Peter Erickson" instead of "Ms. Margaret Lee." Margaret and Peter have just named their first child Michael Lee-Erickson.

1. What are the problems in this situation?

2. Who do you think is unhappy?

3. Is there any solution to these problems?

4. What is the system for women and children's last names in your country?

5. Some other language changes that resulted from the women's movement:

housewife → homemaker

girl, lady → woman

Mrs., Miss → Ms.

Why do you think women wanted these changes?

CONTACT A POINT OF VIEW

 BACKGROUND BUILDING

1. Write the names of the things the woman is carrying in the above illustration.

2. Why is she carrying them? What do these things show?

3. What do you think this reading will be about?

TIMED READING

Read the following point of view and answer the questions in four minutes.

Jane Brown has been married for twelve years. She has three children and lives in a suburb outside Columbus, Ohio. When her youngest child reached school age, Jane decided to go back to work. She felt that she should contribute to the household finances; her salary could make the difference between a financial struggle and a secure financial situation for her family. Jane also felt bored and frustrated in her role as a homemaker and wanted to be more involved in life outside her home.

Jane was worried about her children's adjustment to this new situation, but she arranged for them to go and stay with a woman nearby after school each afternoon. They seem to be happy with the arrangement. The problems seem to be between Jane and her husband, Bill.

When Jane was at home all day, she was able to clean the house, go grocery shopping, wash the clothes, take care of the children, and cook two or three meals each day. She was very busy, of course, but she succeeded in getting everything done. Now these same things need to be done, but Jane has only evenings and early mornings to do them.

Both Jane and Bill are tired when they arrive home at 6:00 P.M. Bill is accustomed to sitting down and reading the paper or watching TV until dinner is ready. This is exactly what Jane feels like doing, but someone has to fix dinner, and Bill expects it to be Jane. Jane is becoming very angry at Bill's attitude. She feels that they should share the household jobs; Bill feels that everything should be the same as it was before Jane went back to work.

Read the following statements carefully to determine whether each is true (T), false (F), or impossible to know (ITK).

1. _____ Jane Brown lives in Columbus, Indiana.

2. _____ Money was one of the reasons why Jane wanted to work.

3. _____ Jane liked her life as a homemaker.

4. _____ Jane was married once before her marriage to Bill.

5. _____ Jane and Bill wake up at 6:00 A.M.

6. _____ Jane wants to relax now after work.

7. _____ Jane is a secretary.

8. _____ They were rich before Jane went back to work.

9. _____ Jane worked at some time before this.

10. _____ Jane and Bill work in the same building.

C VOCABULARY

Circle the letter of the choice with the same meaning as the italicized word.

1. I can't *contribute* any time to your program, but I will be happy to help out with money.

   a. give   b. take   c. have

2. There was a *struggle* between the two children over the football.

   a. fight   b. value   c. plan

3. After they put the money in the bank, they were sure that it was *secure*.

   a. broken   b. safe   c. difficult

4. What an *adjustment* it is to move from Florida to Vermont in January!

   a. problem   b. exclusion   c. changing process

5. We were *tired* because we did not get very much sleep.

   a. exhausted   b. unhappy   c. forced

6. Her *salary* is very high in her new job.

   a. hours   b. status   c. pay

7. They are both very *active* in their school.

   a. different   b. involved   c. absent

8. They may change their plans because they are not happy with the *arrangement*.

   a. situation   b. problems   c. people

9. She was unhappy with her *role* as homemaker.

   a. time   b. position   c. house

10. What were the *effects* of the decision she made?

    a. results   b. reasons   c. causes

D REACT

Read the timed reading again. Work with another student, and answer the following questions. When you are finished, compare your ideas for numbers 5 and 6 with the other students' ideas.

1. What are the problems for Jane Brown?

2. What are the problems for the children?

3. What are the problems for Bill?

4. What are Jane's responsibilities?

5. What are three (3) possible solutions for these problems?

6. What should Jane and Bill do?

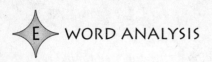

WORD ANALYSIS

PART 1

Choose the appropriate word form for each sentence. Is it a noun, adjective, or verb?

1. vary
   various
   variety

   1. There is little _____ in my job.

2. social
   socialize
   society

   2. I can't believe that you hate to _____.

3. tradition
   traditional

   3. This program is quite _____.

4. industry
   industrial
   industrialize

   4. Pittsburgh is an ___industrial___ city.

5. reside
   residence
   residential

   5. The census states that three people _____ at that address.

6. change
   changeable

   6. The weather here is _____.

7. religion
   religious

   7. She seems like a _____ person.

8. care
   careful

   8. Take _____. You might fall.

9. separate
   separable
   separation

   9. I cannot _____ these two pages.

10. secure
    security

    10. Financial _____ is important to some people.

PART 2

1. Study the meaning of these: Can you think of another example?

dict-	say	pre**dict**	_____
resid-	remain sitting	**resid**ential	_____
tech-	design	**tech**nology	_____
fort-	strong	rein**forc**e	_____
-sta-	firm	e**sta**blished	_____

2. Complete the sentences with one of the above words.

a. Homework can _____ what I study in class.

b. Computer _____ has developed significantly in the last ten years.

c. You can never _____ the weather with 100 percent certainty.

d. The first government _____ laws and procedures.

e. Is this area of the city commercial or _____?

Female Executives and Their Families

How Are Home Responsibilities Handled?

Chores	Wife	Shared	Husband	Can't Say	Children	Wife	Shared	Husband	Can't Say
Paying the bills	54%	25%	21%	*	Shopping for their clothes	70%	17%	3%	10%
Seeing that the laundry is done	52	28	7	13	Managing their excursions and activities	37	46	5	12
Planning meals and shopping for food	47	41	8	4	Tending to them at home when they are ill	30	49	5	16
Planning investments	24	60	15	1	Disciplining them	13	73	4	10

*Less than one percent.

Reprinted by permission of *Wall Street Journal*, © Dow Jones & Company, Inc. All rights reserved.

FIGURE 13

F SKIMMING/SCANNING

Answer the following questions about Figure 13 on page 189.

1. Skim the chart. What does it show? _____

_____

2. Which chore do men and women share most often?

_____

3. Who usually pays the bills? _____

4. Which chores do men rarely have primary responsibility for?

_____

5. Which responsibility for children do women usually handle?

_____

6. Which responsibility for children do men and women share most often?

_____

7. Does this information represent the average American family?

_____

8. How would you fill in the numbers on this chart if we were talking about your family? Is this typical of your culture?

How Are Home Responsibilities Handled?

Chores	Wife	Shared	Husband	Can't Say	Children	Wife	Shared	Husband	Can't Say
Paying the bills					Shopping for their clothes				
Seeing that the laundry is done					Managing their excursions and activities				
Planning meals and shopping for food					Tending to them at home when they are ill				
Planning investments					Disciplining them				

FIGURE 14

9. How would you *like* to see responsibilities shared?

_____

LOOK BACK

A VOCABULARY

Circle the letter of the choice that best completes each sentence.

1. The young man never questioned anything and did everything in the same way that his parent did. He was very __.

   a. uncivilized   b. traditional   c. divorced

2. My __ to the group was small, but they were happy to have help.

   a. contribution   b. establishment   c. solution

3. The __ of cities in the West was important to early Americans.

   a. area   b. establishment   c. responsibility

4. An understanding of the past or a(n) __ view is important for people today.

   a. ironic   b. Protestant   c. historical

5. The worker was good at his job and did it with __.

   a. ease   b. factors   c. lifestyle

6. The army was losing the struggle against the enemy and needed __, other groups of fighters, and ammunition.

   a. society   b. exhaustion   c. reinforcements

7. She was very active in politics. Her __ resulted in a government job.

   a. environment   b. involvement   c. advantage

8. The politician thanked her __ for their help.

   a. supporters   b. factors   c. couples

9. Early settlers found the __ very difficult.

   a. land   b. environment   c. society

10. When should we go on our picnic? Time, weather, and hunger are the three __ to think about.

    a. inventions   b. positions   c. factors

MATCHING

Find the word or phrase in column B that has a similar meaning to a word in column A. Write the letter of that word or phrase next to the word in column A.

	A		B
1. _____	isolated	a.	job
2. _____	sense	b.	diversity
3. _____	active	c.	separated
4. _____	tired	d.	meet
5. _____	encounter	e.	exhausted
6. _____	position	f.	feeling
7. _____	variety	g.	involved
8. _____	secure	h.	only one
9. _____	alone	i.	safe
10. _____	arrange	j.	organize

C SYNTHESIS

Work together.

1. Recently in Boston, a woman was arrested in a men's exercise room at a city health club where the men's and the women's areas are segregated. The woman refused to leave the men's exercise room because the equipment was better, and the weights were heavier than those on the women's side. It seems that the woman was a serious body builder. When the woman refused to leave, the police came, and the woman was taken away. What do you think should happen?

2. In a group, discuss the role of women in your country. Have there been changes in the past twenty years? Consider:

   work   education

   status   home responsibilities

   sports   relationships with men

   religious life

3. Choose one of the following topics. With a partner, make a list of arguments both for or against the topic you chose. Have a debate with partners on the other side of the same debate. Let the class decide on the winner.
   a. Women with children should have jobs outside the home.
   b. Women should be in government.
   c. Women should have the same rights as men.

11 TAXES, TAXES, AND MORE TAXES

A FIRST LOOK

 BACKGROUND BUILDING

Look at the picture on the preceding page. The man is giving money to someone. Who is the man taking the money? What does that man represent? The man is paying taxes. Why do people pay taxes?

Before reading the article, decide if these statements are true or false.

1. _____ In the United States, everyone pays taxes to the national government.

2. _____ All states charge taxes.

3. _____ The amount of money that you pay in taxes is 10 percent of your income.

4. _____ State tax laws are the same in every state.

5. _____ Americans have to pay taxes on their cars.

B TOPIC

Skim the reading. Write the topic of each paragraph on the lines below.

1. _____

2. _____

3. _____

4. _____

5. _____

6. _____

7. _____

Now read.

TAXES, TAXES, AND MORE TAXES

1   Americans often say that there are only two things a person can be sure of in life: death and taxes. Americans do not have a corner on the "death" market, but many Americans feel that the United States leads the world with the worst taxes.

2   Taxes consist of the money that people pay to support their government. There are generally three levels of government in the United States: federal, state, and city; therefore, there are three types of taxes.

3   Salaried people who earn more than four to five thousand dollars per year must pay a certain percentage of their salaries to the federal (national) government. The percentage varies for individuals. It depends on their salaries. The federal government has several levels of income tax starting at 15 percent. These percentages are based on how much a person earns. The percentage increases as a person's income increases. For example, if a person earns $20,000, she pays 15 percent. If she earns $40,000, she pays 20 percent. With the high cost of taxes, people are not very happy on April 15 when federal taxes are due.

4   The second tax is for the state government: New York, California, North Dakota, or any of the other forty-seven states. Most states have an income tax similar to that of the federal government, but the percentage for the state tax is lower. Many states have a sales tax, which is a percentage charged on any item that you buy in that state. For example, a person might want to buy a package of gum for twenty-five cents. If there is a sales tax of 8 percent in that state, the cost of the gum is twenty-seven cents. This figure includes the sales tax. Some states use income tax in addition to sales tax to raise their revenues. The state tax laws are diverse and confusing.

5   The third tax is for the city. This tax comes in two forms: property tax (residents who own a home have to pay taxes on it) and excise tax, which is a tax on vehicles in a city. The cities utilize these funds for education, police and fire departments, public works (including street repairs, water, and sanitation), and municipal buildings.

6   Besides these three taxes, Americans also have to pay Social Security taxes so that they will have income from the government when they retire. Many people are worried that this tax will not provide enough money because of the large number of retirees in the near future.

7   Americans pay high taxes; one study says that they are working two days each week just to pay their taxes. People always complain about taxes. They often protest that the government misuses their tax dollars. They say that it spends too much on useless and impractical programs. Although Americans have conflicting views on many issues—religious, racial, cultural, and political—they tend to agree on one subject: Taxes are too high.

REACT

Look at the reading again. Choose one sentence that surprised you. Write down the sentence, and then explain to a partner why it surprised you.

 D SCANNING/VOCABULARY

PART 1

*Scan the reading for these words. Write the number of the line where you find them. Then compare the meaning in the sentence to the meaning of the word(s) on the right. Are the words similar or different? Write **similar** or **different** on the line.*

	LINE NUMBER		SIMILAR OR DIFFERENT
1. consist of	5	are made of	S
2. due		payable	
3. include		keep out	d
4. repairs	2	rebuilding	S
5. complain about		say good things about	D
6. spend		save	
7. misuse	36	use well	D
8. conflicting		similar	D
9. tend to		seem to	S
10. subject		opinion	D

PART 2

Find a word in the reading that has a meaning similar to the following. The line number is given.

1. line 6	national	
2. line 7	kinds	
3. line 10	changes	in
4. line 22	contains	
5. line 23	income	
6. line 29	city	
7. line 36	disagree strongly	
8. line 37	not realistic	
9. line 38	opinion	
10. line 38	problems	

READING COMPREHENSION

Circle the letter of the choice that best completes each sentence.

1. In the United States, there are generally __ basic types of taxes, plus Social Security.

   a. two   b. three   c. four

2. A person must pay federal taxes if that person __.

   a. has a   b. lives in certain   c. earns more than a
   part-time job   states   few thousand dollars

3. There are __ basic types of city taxes.

   a. three   b. two   c. four

4. Some states tax items that a person buys. This is a(n) __ tax.

   a. income   b. sales   c. excise

5. State sales taxes __ in different states.

   a. are fixed   b. are based   c. vary greatly
                         on income

6. Cities get tax money from two different sources: homeowners and __.

   a. property   b. municipal   c. drivers
                        employees

7. Americans have to work two days out of every five to __.

   a. pay the   b. relax   c. misuse their taxes
   government

8. Each of the __ states probably has individual tax laws.

   a. forty-seven   b. three   c. fifty

9. A person who earns $17,000 pays 15 percent of it in federal taxes. A person who earns $30,000 probably pays __.

   a. 15 percent   b. a lower   c. a higher percentage
   also   percentage

10. The author thinks that we can be certain about two things: __.

    a. useless and   b. taxes and death   c. sales tax and
    impractical   income tax
    programs

LOOK AGAIN

A VOCABULARY

Circle the letter of the choice that best completes each sentence.

1. Taxes must be paid on a certain day. They are __ on that day.
   a. sure   b. due   c. raised

2. A(n) __ person earns an income.
   a. impractical   b. salaried   c. resident

3. The amount of income tax a person pays __ his or her salary.
   a. depends on   b. earns   c. increases

4. People today are often careless, and they __ our national resources.
   a. spend   b. complain about   c. misuse

5. You cannot agree. He has his __, and you have yours.
   a. aspect   b. view   c. protest

6. The United States is a country of immigrants. There are many __ of Americans.
   a. percentages   b. types   c. issues

7. When Americans don't like what the government is doing, they usually __.
   a. include   b. protest   c. reinforce

8. When people from warm countries visit cold areas, they usually __ about the weather.
   a. vary   b. complain   c. tend

9. It is __ for a person who doesn't drive to work to buy a car.
   a. conflicting   b. impractical   c. confusing

10. Energy is one of the most important __ of this century.
    a. issues   b. views   c. solutions

READING COMPREHENSION

Fill out the information in the outline.

1. Americans can be sure of two things in life: _____
   and _____.

2. There are generally three types of taxes in addition to Social Security
   taxes:

   a._____

   b._____

   c._____

3. Income taxes vary for individuals.

   a.Those who earn less _____.

   b.Those who earn more _____.

4. Many individual states also charge taxes. Some have _____,

   and others have _____.

5. City taxes fall into two forms:

   a._____ for _____

   b._____ for _____

6. There is also a social security tax. This is for _____.

7. When people complain about taxes, they say that . . . .

   a._____.

   b._____.

   Americans generally agree _____.

C THINK ABOUT IT

Discuss the answers to these questions with your classmates.

In the United States, as in many countries, the citizens do not enjoy paying taxes, so collecting taxes can be a problem. The Swedish government has an interesting solution. Each year it publishes a book with a list of all individual taxpayers who earn the equivalent of $15,000 or more and each married couple who earns $20,000 or more. The book is similar to the telephone book. In this way, everyone knows how much money you make and how much you pay in taxes.

This system would not be useful in the United States. Americans are very private about many things, especially how much money they make. This would not be a good system of keeping track of taxes. Are salaries private in your country? Is it impolite to ask a person how much money he or she makes?

Running a government is very expensive. In the United States, most of the money comes from taxes—both from individuals and from corporations. Another part comes from social security payments (about 7 percent of an individual's salary). Other money comes from borrowing. Figure 15 indicates where the money in the 1993 budget came from, and Figure 16 shows how the money was spent.

U. S. Budget

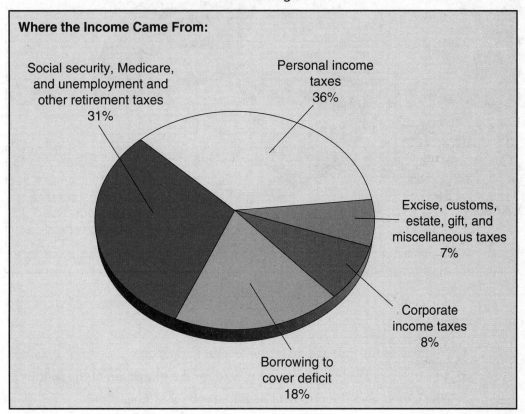

Where the Income Came From:

Social security, Medicare, and unemployment and other retirement taxes
31%

Personal income taxes
36%

Excise, customs, estate, gift, and miscellaneous taxes
7%

Corporate income taxes
8%

Borrowing to cover deficit
18%

FIGURE 15

1. What percentage of the U.S. budget comes from income taxes?

2. Who contributes more to the federal government—corporations or individuals?

3. How much of the federal budget comes from Social Security and related taxes?

4. What percentage comes from borrowing (taking money now and paying it back later)?

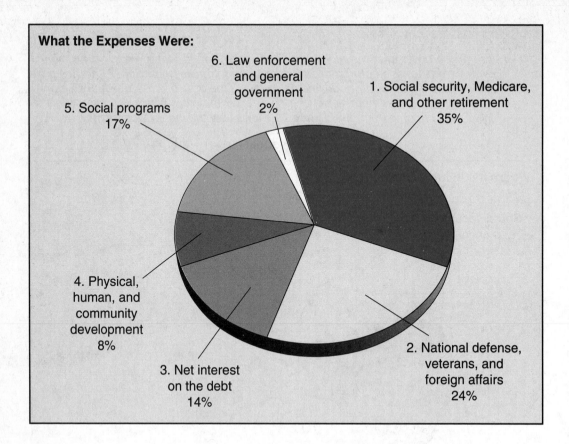

What the Expenses Were:

6. Law enforcement and general government 2%

5. Social programs 17%

1. Social security, Medicare, and other retirement 35%

4. Physical, human, and community development 8%

3. Net interest on the debt 14%

2. National defense, veterans, and foreign affairs 24%

FIGURE 16

1. Where does the largest part of the federal budget go?
2. How much of the federal budget is used for the protection of the country?
3. Which area does the president's salary probably come from?
4. What percentage of the federal budget supports retired people?
5. What percentage is used to pay interest on borrowing?
6. After comparing income and expenses for the U.S. government, what surprises you?

CONTACT A POINT OF VIEW

INCOME

 BACKGROUND BUILDING

Figure 17 below illustrates part of a page from the U.S. tax forms. Imagine that you are a single person who earns $29,125 in taxable income. What do you have to pay the federal government? Scan the table to find out. What percentage of your income is that figure?

1994 Tax Table—*Continued*

If line 37 (taxable income) is—		And you are—				If line 37 (taxable income) is—		And you are—				If line 37 (taxable income) is—		And you are—			
At least	But less than	Single	Married filing jointly	Married filing sepa-rately	Head of a house-hold	At least	But less than	Single	Married filing jointly	Married filing sepa-rately	Head of a house-hold	At least	But less than	Single	Married filing jointly	Married filing sepa-rately	Head of a house-hold
				Your tax is—						Your tax is—						Your tax is—	
23,000						**26,000**						**29,000**					
23,000	23,050	3,490	3,454	3,977	3,454	26,000	23,050	4,330	3,904	4,817	3,904	29,000	29,050	5,170	4,354	5,657	4,354
23,050	23,100	3,504	3,461	3,991	3,461	26,050	23,100	4,344	3,911	4,831	3,911	29,050	29,100	5,184	4,361	5,671	4,361
23,100	23,150	3,518	3,469	4,005	3,469	26,100	23,150	4,358	3,919	4,845	3,919	29,100	29,150	5,198	4,369	5,685	4,369
23,150	23,200	3,532	3,476	4,019	3,476	26,150	23,200	4,372	3,926	4,859	3,926	29,150	29,200	5,212	4,376	5,699	4,376

Source: Internal Revenue Service

FIGURE 17

TIMED READING

Read the following point of view and answer the questions in four minutes.

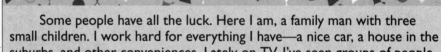

Some people have all the luck. Here I am, a family man with three small children. I work hard for everything I have—a nice car, a house in the suburbs, and other conveniences. Lately on TV, I've seen groups of people on welfare who complain that they can't get by on their incomes. How do you think I feel? People on welfare don't work, and they get money from the government. Who pays the bills? I do. Twenty-five percent of my salary goes to taxes: federal and state taxes. Then, of course, there is the property tax on the house and the excise tax on the car, and, of course, Social Security. I've had it with taxes. I probably work two days a week to pay all my taxes. It really angers me that I can't have the kind of life I deserve—the kind of life that I have worked for.

The president says that the government is trying to cut back, and then the budget goes up. The local politicians say that they need more money for highway repairs, and then they vote a salary increase for themselves. The town selectmen say we need a new elementary school. We just can't afford it. Who helps me when the kids need new shoes? No one. People used to say that the rich get richer and the poor get poorer. Now I am beginning to think that the people in the middle class are the real losers.

Read the following statements carefully to determine whether each is true (T), false (F), or impossible to know (ITK).

1. _____ This man lives in the city.

2. _____ More than twenty-five percent of his salary goes to taxes.

3. _____ He has three older children.

4. _____ He pays taxes on his home.

5. _____ Money for education comes from the state.

6. _____ He is on welfare.

7. _____ He is from the upper class.

8. _____ He thinks that the middle class is lucky.

9. _____ Local politicians have high salaries.

10. _____ The president is trying to cut spending.

C VOCABULARY

Circle the letter of the choice with the same meaning as the italicized word(s).

1. I can't have the kind of life I *deserve*.
   - a. should have
   - b. can have
   - c. had

2. It *angers* him that he can't have an easy life.
   - a. confuses
   - b. upsets
   - c. worries

3. We should not *complain* about taxes. They are necessary.
   - a. feel unhappy
   - b. say bad things
   - c. care

4. The budget *goes up* yearly.
   - a. decreases
   - b. increases
   - c. changes

5. These are some of our *local* politicians.
   - a. far away
   - b. misplaced
   - c. from the area

6. The government is trying to *cut back* spending.
   - a. increase
   - b. decrease
   - c. maintain

7. People in the middle class are the real *losers*.
   - a. people who don't gain
   - b. people who don't lose
   - c. people who complain

8. There are many *conveniences* in American homes.
   - a. interesting things
   - b. affordable objects
   - c. helpful things

D REACT

Work with a committee of three or four students to plan a budget for your country. Take the roles of the president, the minister of defense, the minister of human services, and the minister of transportation. Fill out the pie chart on the next page to show how you would organize your budget. Be prepared to present your budget to the public (the other students in your class).

_____ defense   _____ health care

_____ welfare   _____ daycare centers

_____ unemployment compensation   _____ roads and highways

_____ social security   _____ public transportation

_____ education   _____ energy research

_____ old-age homes   _____ pollution control

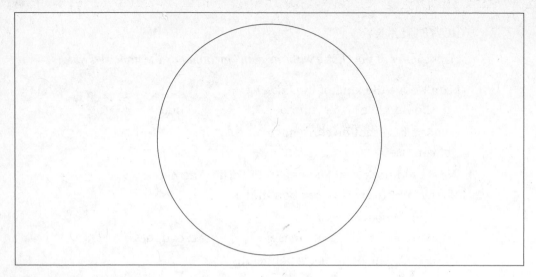

E ▸ WORD ANALYSIS

*Read the following information about **adverbs** and **adjectives**, and then complete the exercise. Decide if the italicized words in the sentences are adverbs or adjectives.*

Adjectives explain <u>nouns</u> more clearly. He is a *slow* speaker. *(noun)*

Adverbs explain <u>verbs</u> more clearly: He speaks *slowly*. *(verb)*

Adverbs can also explain <u>adjectives</u> or other <u>adverbs</u> more clearly:

She speaks *very slowly*. She is a *very slow* speaker. *(adverb)* *(adjective)*

	ADVERB	ADJECTIVE
1. She is always *independent*.	___	___
2. His ideas are *practically* impossible.	___	___
3. She arrives late *consistently*.	___	___
4. Those cars are really *fast*.	___	___
5. He drives *fast*.	___	___
6. They are a *typical* American family.	___	___
7. I *always* get up late.	___	___
8. *Lately*, I have been thinking about a vacation.	___	___
9. The style of her letter was very *formal*.	___	___
10. *Naturally*, she doesn't want to give up her job.	___	___

LOOK BACK

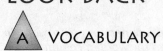

A VOCABULARY

Circle the letter of the choice that best completes each sentence.

1. He has many strong ideas. He is very __.
    a. opinionated   b. changeable   c. impractical

2. We cannot decide; we __ about everything.
    a. raise   b. avoid   c. disagree

3. Food is not __ in some states.
    a. graduated   b. taxable   c. variable

4. My watch is very __.
    a. valuable   b. conflicting   c. solvable

5. He gave me the wrong directions. I was __.
    a. impractical   b. misinformed   c. directed

6. My telephone bill is __ tomorrow.
    a. paid   b. due   c. differentiated

7. She __ happy, but I'm not sure.
    a. tends to be   b. certainly is   c. seems to be

8. He is a good father; he is very __ his children.
    a. supportive of   b. dependent on   c. uncertain of

9. The federal government __ many educational programs.
    a. consists of   b. funds   c. spends

10. The students were very dissatisfied. We listened to their __.
    a. experiences   b. complaints   c. models

B MATCHING

Find the word or phrase in column B that has a similar meaning to a word in column A. Write the letter of that word or phrase next to the word in column A.

	A		B
1. _____	impractical	a. property
2. _____	possessions	b. complain
3. _____	seem to	c. useless
4. _____	protest	d. utilize
5. _____	comprise	e. extra
6. _____	additional	f. appear to
7. _____	national	g. include
8. _____	kind	h. federal
9. _____	repair	i. type
10. _____	use	j. fix

C SYNTHESIS

Work together.

1. Take a survey in your class about taxes in different countries. How are taxes determined? Compare the percentage of taxes in your country to those of your classmates' countries.

2. Go to the local library, and ask for tax forms and information. These are easy to get from January 1 until April 15, the due date for taxes. Look up the tax payment for someone who earns $40,000 taxable income; what percent is it?

3. The following chart shows tax revenues per person in selected countries in 1991. The figures are given in U.S. dollars.

Australia	$ 5,050
Canada	8,190
Denmark	12,219
Japan	8,419
Portugal	2,487
Sweden	14,628
United States	6,550

a. Of these seven countries, which country has the highest tax figure per person?

b. Which has the lowest?

c. Do you know any reasons why taxes are high in these countries?

d. What kinds of services or programs does your country's government provide for its citizens?

D VOCABULARY PREVIEW

What shorter words can you see in these words from Chapter 12?

1. official _____   6. basic _____

2. resultant _____   7. Protestant _____

3. representation _____   8. existence _____

4. breakthrough _____   9. de-emphasize _____

5. intermarriage _____   10. community _____

12 FREEDOM OF RELIGION

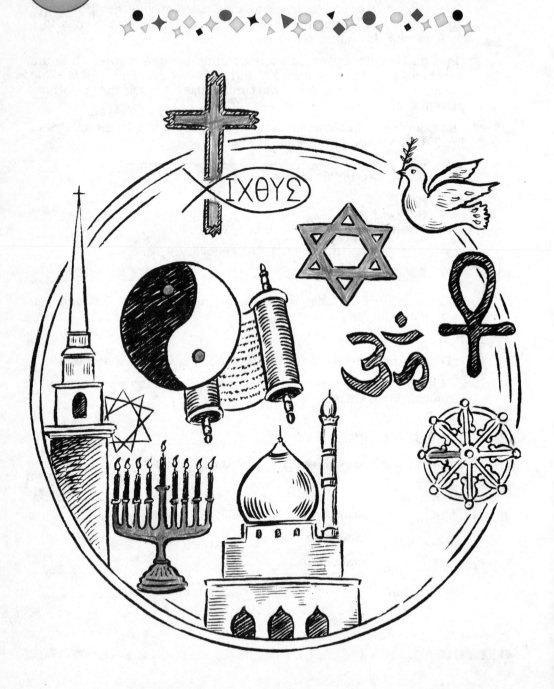

A FIRST LOOK

A BACKGROUND BUILDING

1. Are you familiar with any of the symbols on the preceding page? What religions do they represent?

2. What religions are most common in the United States? How about in your country?

3. Before you read, decide if the following statements are true (T) or false (F). Discuss your answers with your classmates.

   a. _____ Every country should have a national religion.

   b. _____ Everyone in the United States is a Christian.

   c. _____ Roman Catholics are Christians.

   d. _____ Protestants are Christians.

   e. _____ There are 1,500 different religious groups in the United States.

   f. _____ The majority of people in the United States are Protestants.

   g. _____ President John F. Kennedy was Roman Catholic.

   h. _____ Two people of different religions cannot get married in the United States.

   i. _____ Islam is the second largest religion in the world.

   j. _____ People never have trouble in the United States because of their religion.

B TOPIC

Before you begin to read, look at these topics. There is one topic for each paragraph. Look quickly at the reading to find these topics. Do not read every word at this point. Write the number of the paragraph next to the topic of that paragraph.

1. _____ general description of Christianity

2. _____ the Jewish religion

3. _____ the Protestant church

4. _____ historical background for freedom of religion

5. _____ the Roman Catholic church

6. _____ traditional feelings about non-Protestant beliefs

7. _____ recent changes

8. _____ other religions growing

Now read.

FREEDOM OF RELIGION

1   The first immigrants who came to New England in the 1600s left their own countries for religious reasons. They had religious beliefs different from the accepted beliefs of their countries; they wanted to live in a place where they could be free to have their own beliefs. When they came to establish new communities in the New World, they decided that there would be no official religion. When this new country gained its independence from Britain in 1776, the separation of church and state was one of the basic laws for the United States. This absence of an official national religion and the freedom to believe in whatever one wants to has attracted many new immigrants. In the United States, there are 1,500 different religious groups representing every kind of world religion—Buddhist, Islamic, Baha'i, to name only a few. Many religions also began in the United States, such as the Pentecostal, Mormon, and Christian Science religions. But most of the people in the United States are Christian.

2   Quite simply, Christian means believing in Christ, or Jesus. Christians celebrate Christmas, the birth of Christ, and Easter, the time at which Christians remember Jesus's death and celebrate his rebirth. They think of Sunday as a holy day and worship in churches. In the United States, Christianity can be divided into two major groups: Roman Catholicism and Protestantism. A third group, Orthodoxy, is not as common in the United States.

3   As its name suggests, the Roman Catholic church is based in Rome. It is centered around the authority of one man, the Pope, who is the head of the Roman Catholic church throughout the world. There is a hierarchy of authority and responsibility beginning with the Pope in Rome and ending with the priests who are the heads of the churches in individual neighborhoods and communities.

4   As its name suggests, the Protestant church began as a protest against another church: the Roman Catholic church. Protestant is a very general term; it includes many different church groups, such as Episcopalian, Presbyterian, Lutheran, Methodist, Baptist, and many more. The majority of people in the United States have Protestant backgrounds. However, since there are so many Protestant churches, each with its own traditions, people who are Protestants do not really share similar religious experiences. As opposed to the Roman Catholic church, in which there is a lot of central control, Protestant churches are generally more autonomous, with more control and authority on a local level.

5   Judaism is next in religious preference in the United States. Jews and Christians share many of the same basic principles and beliefs. They both believe in the existence of one God. But whereas Christians believe in Christ, a

5   representation of God on earth, Jews do not believe that God has come to   38
     earth in any form. Jewish people celebrate a weekly holy day from Friday evening 39
     to Saturday evening and worship in synagogues. The head of a synagogue is   40
     called a rabbi. Many Jewish people came to the United States in the first half of 41
     the twentieth century because of religious intolerance in their own countries.   42

6   Islam, the second largest religion in the world, is growing in the United   43
     States, as are many eastern religions such as Buddhism and Hinduism. In every   44
     city, you can see new mosques, temples, and other religious buildings.   45

7   Although freedom of religion is an important concept in the United States,   46
     religious intolerance sometimes occurs. Because the majority of early   47
     Americans were Protestant, there has sometimes been discrimination against   48
     new immigrants, such as the Irish and Italians, who were Roman Catholic.   49
     Protestants were reluctant to share their traditional power with members of   50
     other churches or religions. The year 1960 marked a breakthrough in the   51
     religious tolerance of the country, when John F. Kennedy, a Roman Catholic,   52
     became the first non-Protestant President of the United States.   53

8   Recently, there has been a large increase in the number of Americans who   54
     consider themselves fundamental Christians: those who rely closely on the Bible 55
     to guide their lives. On the other hand, there has also been an increase in the   56
     number of agnostics, those who do not have a preference for a particular   57
     religion. A recent study indicates that even among those who indicate a religious 58
     preference, many do not participate actively in religious services.   59

REACT

Find some information in the reading that surprised you. Discuss it with a
partner.

D SCANNING/VOCABULARY

Find a synonym for the word given in the paragraph indicated.

Paragraph 1

1. traditional   _____
2. build   _____
3. sanctioned by government _____
4. division   _____
5. essential   _____
6. lack   _____
7. interested   _____

Paragraph 3

8. power and control   _____
9. leader   _____
10. power structure   _____

Paragraph 4

11. greatest number   _____

READING COMPREHENSION

Circle the letter of the choice that best completes each sentence.

1. Most people in the United States have __ backgrounds.
   a. Protestant   b. Roman Catholic   c. Jewish

2. The early Americans were __.
   a. Protestant   b. Roman Catholic   c. Jewish

3. Many Jewish people came to the United States __.
   a. in the 1600s   b. before 1950   c. in the 1950s

4. According to the author, __ is more hierarchical than other religions.
   a. the Jewish   b. Protestantism   c. Roman Catholicism
      religion

5. According to the author, there __ religious discrimination in the United States.
   a. is now no   b. has sometimes   c. never used to be
                          been

6. Protestants belong to __.
   a. many   b. the Roman   c. similar churches
      different   Catholic church
      churches

7. The United States has __ religion.
   a. an official   b. no   c. no official

8. __ is the second largest religion in the world.
   a. Judaism   b. Islam   c. Catholicism

9. In the Protestant church, there is __ control on the local level.
   a. no   b. a lot of   c. rarely

10. According to the reading, even if people say that they belong to a particular religion, they sometimes __ participate in services.
    a. don't like to   b. do not   c. cannot

LOOK AGAIN

A VOCABULARY

Circle the letter of the choice that best completes each sentence.

1. Churches, synagogues, and mosques are places where people __.
   a. believe   b. worship   c. attract

2. Most large organizations have a __ of power and authority.
   a. hierarchy   b. reluctance   c. reason

3. My friend is the __ of the department. She is the supervisor.
   a. head   b. representation   c. priest

4. A director in a company has the __ to make decisions.
   a. hierarchy   b. persecution   c. authority

5. The two products are very similar. The __ difference is their cost.
   a. traditional   b. fundamental   c. close

6. He never thinks about his religious __.
   a. level   b. head   c. beliefs

7. The mayor of a city is not involved in the federal government. The mayor is in __ government.
   a. national   b. individual   c. local

8. The president's wife was the __ head of the company.
   a. unofficial   b. attracted   c. raised

9. The town, not the state, had control of its own policies. The town was __.
   a. autonomous   b. tolerant   c. centered

10. We decided not to go running __ it was raining out.
    a. throughout   b. since   c. as opposed to

B READING COMPREHENSION

Complete the outline of the reading.

I. Introduction

_____

_____

II. _____

_____

_____

_____

III. _____

_____

_____

IV. _____

_____

V. _____

_____

_____

VI. _____

_____

_____

VII. _____

_____

_____

VIII. _____

_____

_____

C THINK ABOUT IT

Answer the following questions.

1. Does your country have an official religion?
2. Do you know of any official religions of any countries?
3. What are the countries and the religions?
4. Work with your classmates to complete this chart. List any religions.

	RELIGION 1	RELIGION 2	RELIGION 3	RELIGION 4
Name	_____	_____	_____	_____
Religious Leaders	_____	_____	_____	_____
Special Building(s)	_____	_____	_____	_____
Book(s)	_____	_____	_____	_____
Holidays/Celebrations	_____	_____	_____	_____
Rules	_____	_____	_____	_____
	_____	_____	_____	_____
Beliefs	_____	_____	_____	_____
	_____	_____	_____	_____

D READING

Study the information in the graph, and answer the following questions.

Religious Preference in the United States *(in percentage)*					
Year	*Protestant*	*Catholic*	*Jewish*	*Other*	*None*
1957	66	26	3	1	3
1967	67	25	3	3	2
1975	62	27	2	4	6
1980	61	28	2	2	7
1985	57	28	2	4	9
1991	56	25	2	6	11

Source: U.S. Statistical Abstracts, 1994

FIGURE 18

1. Which religion do the majority of people prefer?
2. Has religion become more popular or less? How do you know?
3. Are you surprised by these numbers? If so, what surprises you?

CONTACT A POINT OF VIEW

 BACKGROUND BUILDING

Answer the following questions.

1. Are you very religious? Do you pray or go to /church/mosque/temple/ synagogue? How often?

2. Do your parents and family have the same religious beliefs as you do?

Read the following paragraphs and answer the questions in four minutes.

Kathy Robinson is a very religious person. She feels that her relationship with God is the most important thing in her life. Her closest friends are also very devout, and they meet once a week to pray together and to talk about their religious beliefs and experiences.

Kathy is a management trainee at a large bank. When she went to work at the bank last year, she met an interesting man, Bob Thomas. Everyone in Kathy's department thought Bob was amazing because he became a top manager so quickly. Kathy liked him because he was kind to the management trainees and was always available to help them with questions and problems. After Kathy had been at the bank three months, Bob left Kathy's bank to become a vice-president at another bank. Everyone was sorry to see him leave.

When Bob started his new job, he called Kathy and invited her to lunch. Soon they were going out for dinner and movies as well. They had a lot in common, and Kathy soon realized that Bob was in love with her. She also feels very strongly about him, but there is one problem. Bob is not a religious person. He never prays or even thinks about God. Bob wants to marry Kathy, but Kathy, even though she loves Bob too, thinks that she should stop seeing him.

Read the following statements carefully to determine whether each is true (T), false (F), or impossible to know (ITK).

1. _____ Kathy's closest friends are very religious people.

2. _____ Kathy and Bob work at the same bank.

3. _____ Kathy and Bob have known each other for three years.

4. _____ Bob was successful at Kathy's bank.

5. _____ Kathy is a manager in the bank.

6. _____ Kathy and Bob share a lot of interests.

7. _____ Kathy's friends think she should stop seeing Bob.

8. _____ Her religious beliefs are more important than marriage to Kathy.

9. _____ Bob did not ask Kathy out when they worked together.

10. _____ Kathy wants to marry someone who shares her religious beliefs.

C VOCABULARY

Circle the letter of the choice with the same meaning as the italicized word(s).

1. They are *devout* Christians.
   a. serious　　　　　b. very religious　　　c. unhappy

2. We are *praying* that he will recover from his injuries.
   a. asking God　　　b. trying to help　　　c. believing in God

3. This is *amazing* news!
   a. serious　　　　　b. interesting　　　　c. surprising

4. We don't have much *in common*.
   a. normally　　　　b. typically　　　　　c. of shared interest

5. I'll be *available* between 10 and 12 o'clock in my office.
   a. willing to help you　　b. able to go out　　c. busy working

6. I don't discuss my *beliefs* very often.
   a. thoughts　　　　b. things I think　　　c. what society is
   　　　　　　　　　　　 are true　　　　　　　convinced of

7. Which *department* do you work in?
   a. division of　　　b. field of work　　　c. government office
   　　a company

8. Becky and Karl are *seeing* each other.
   a. watching　　　　b. visiting　　　　　c. going out with

9. I didn't *realize* how you felt about this.
   a. understand　　　b. think　　　　　　c. remember

10. They are enrolled in a computer *training* program.
   a. instruction　　　b. design　　　　　c. teaching

D REACT

Discuss the following questions with your classmates.

1. How important is it to marry someone who shares your feelings about religion? Why?

2. If Kathy and Bob get married, what problems might they face?

3. What do you think they should do?

4. Bob didn't ask Kathy out until he was working at a different bank. Perhaps the bank had a rule against dating or marrying someone you work with. Is this rule common in your country?

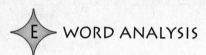

WORD ANALYSIS

Choose the appropriate word form for each sentence. Is it an adjective or an adverb?

ADJECTIVE	ADVERB
natural	naturally
formal	formally

1. careful
   carefully

2. traditional
   traditionally

3. essential
   essentially

4. serious
   seriously

5. perfect
   perfectly

6. social
   socially

7. cultural
   culturally

8. vast
   vastly

9. minimal
   minimally

10. ironic
    ironically

1. He spoke _____ about the problem.

2. My father dresses very _____.

3. It is _____ to study all aspects of the problem.

4. She is _____ about her work.

5. That design is _____ beautiful.

6. He is nervous _____.

7. Lifestyles vary _____.

8. Our opinions are _____ different.

9. That change is _____.

10. That play was extremely _____.

LOOK BACK

A VOCABULARY

Circle the letter of the choice that best completes each sentence.

1. I don't know very much about his __, but his present behavior is more important to me.
   a. autonomy   b. background   c. authority

2. The biggest part of a group of people is the __.
   a. minority   b. majority   c. population

3. What is the __ for a marriage between two people of different religions or races?
   a. term   b. intermarriage   c. portion

4. There wasn't any sugar __, so I used honey.
   a. seeing   b. autonomous   c. available

5. I use a yellow pen to __ the important sentences in the book.
   a. experience   b. emphasize   c. breakthrough

6. My __ idea is the same as yours; we just disagree about the details.
   a. unsuccessful   b. local   c. basic

7. There is no __ between the different living areas of the house. It is all one big room.
   a. discrimination b. separation   c. independence

8. Which church do you __ in?
   a. worship   b. head   c. occur

9. The discovery of electricity was a great __.
   a. breakthrough   b. belief   c. reference

10. How much money do you need to __ a business?
    a. see   b. discriminate   c. establish

B MATCHING

Find the word or phrase in column B that has a similar meaning to a word in column A. Write the letter of that word or phrase next to the word in column A.

	A		B
1. _____	tolerance	a.	idea
2. _____	decline	b.	someone learning in a business
3. _____	occur	c.	acceptance
4. _____	separation	d.	because
5. _____	concept	e.	self-government
6. _____	belief	f.	word
7. _____	local	g.	decrease
8. _____	term	h.	happen
9. _____	trainee	i.	principle
10. _____	since	j.	split
11. _____	autonomy	k.	near

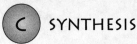

C SYNTHESIS

Work together.

1. Do you feel that religion affects everyday life? If so, how?

2. Is religion becoming more or less important in your country?

3. Interview someone from one of the religions you have discussed or read about in this chapter. Work with your classmates to develop interview questions.

CONCLUSION:
A CHANGING AMERICA

A BACKGROUND BUILDING

Work together. *In a small group, brainstorm areas of American life you have read about and discussed in this book. Write down as many as you can.*

_____

_____

_____

_____

_____

_____

B READING

Now read.

A CHANGING AMERICA

1   The United States is similar to most other countries in the world. Like other countries, the United States is changing at a very fast pace. Our values and our people are changing, and many people are afraid of these changes.

2   The 1950s was the last decade of calm for this country. The fifties was a time of convertibles, poodle skirts, and hula hoops. It was a problem-free time when life was predictable and you had no fear of leaving your door unlocked. Since that time there have been many changes in the country.

3   The American population is changing. The equal rights movement of the 1960s opened doors for American women and men of all races and ethnic backgrounds. Minorities and women have more opportunities than ever before.

4   Americans are also getting older. The number of senior citizens continues to increase, while the number of babies is declining. Families may be having fewer children because of birth control, the high cost of raising children, or uncertainty about the future. On the other hand, teenage mothers are becoming more and more common.

5   Americans are moving, too. They are going to the warmer parts of the country, to some of the older cities, and to some large suburban areas. When they move, they often leave their home towns and extended families behind. They have to create new friends wherever they go. Sometimes the office becomes the new neighborhood, and people at the office become our friends and "neighbors."

(line numbers) 1 2 3 4 5 6 7 8 9 10 11 12 13 14 15 16 17 18 19 20 21

6   We are a wealthy country, but our wealth is not evenly distributed. We still have homeless people, hungry children, and crime. Some immigrants have the idea that America is a "land of opportunities." Hard work still brings great results, as evidenced by the newest immigrants, but unemployment is a problem in many parts of the country. For many Americans, the United States is not a land of easy success.   22–27

7   American women are working more, but they still do not have the same opportunities for equal salaries and advancement as men. They often find that they have two jobs now: taking care of the house and the children as well as working at the office.   28–31

8   Racial discrimination is illegal; every American citizen is guaranteed equal opportunity before the law, but prejudice and fear of other groups still persist. African Americans continue to earn less than whites throughout the work force, and certain center cities have become almost totally African American because of the movement of whites to the suburbs. These forms of discrimination and segregation are almost impossible to control.   32–37

9   Government decisions in Washington greatly affect individuals. Religion is still a private issue, but there are many areas such as school prayer and abortion where the government is making decisions about private, ethical matters.   38–40

10   Americans worry about the same issues as other people around the world, about their children, and how their lives will be. They worry about crime, drugs, and terrorism, and about too much government control. They know that this time is a period of immense change, but they also realize that change can be beneficial even if it is difficult. They face many uncertainties, but perhaps the pioneer spirit that built the country will also help Americans to change, improve, and adapt to the future.   41–47

REACT

Look at your list from Exercise A and see how it compares to the article. Did you write down any concepts that the author did not mention? Did the author mention any ideas that you did not think of?

C VOCABULARY

Find each of the following words in the reading and write the line number where you found it. Then write a word or phrase with a similar meaning on the line.

	LINE NUMBER	SIMILAR WORD
1. pace	_____	_____
2. afraid	_____	_____
3. calm	_____	_____
4. predictable	_____	_____
5. opportunities	_____	_____
6. extended	_____	_____
7. create	_____	_____
8. distributed	_____	_____
9. homeless	_____	_____
10. evidenced	_____	_____
11. worry	_____	_____
12. terrorism	_____	_____
13. control	_____	_____
14. immense	_____	_____
15. realize	_____	_____

D WORD FORMS: REVIEW

Choose the appropriate word form for each sentence. Is it a noun, adjective, adverb, or verb?

general
generally
generalize
generalization

individual
individually
individualize
individualization

differ
different
differently
difference

free
freely
freedom

simple
simply
simplify
simplification

1. We _____ go home at about 5:30 P.M.

2. It is easy to _____ about things that are unfamiliar to you.

3. The teacher talked to each student _____.

4. Your _____ opinion is important to me.

5. We do things very _____.

6. What _____ does it make?

7. May I speak _____?

8. You are _____ to do whatever you want.

9. I know a _____ solution to the problem.

10. I think that I need to _____ my life.

E SYNTHESIS

Work together.

1. Many of the issues mentioned in this concluding reading concern problems in the United States, but similar problems exist throughout the world. Choose one issue that you have read about, and discuss it in relation to your own country.

2. Role play. Choose one of the topics in this book. Think of a conflict that could develop when people disagree. Take roles in a "problem" situation; have your classmates watch your role play and then help to find possible solutions to the conflict.